# Bicycling with Children

# Bicycling with Children

## A Complete How-To Guide

TRUDY E. BELL
with Roxana K. Bell

THE
MOUNTAINEERS

Published by
The Mountaineers
1001 SW Klickitat Way, Suite 201
Seattle, WA 98134

First edition, 1999

Published simultaneously in Great Britain by Cordee, 3a DeMontfort Street, Leicester, England, LE1 7HD

Manufactured in Canada

Edited by Deborah Kaufmann
All photographs by the author unless otherwise noted
Cover and book design by Kristy L. Welch
Layout by Kristy L. Welch
Illustrations by Scott Gaudette

Cover photograph: Adventure Photo
Frontispiece: PhotoDisc, Inc.

*Library of Congress Cataloging-in-Publication Data*
Bell, Trudy E.
    Bicycling with children : a complete how-to guide / Trudy E.
Bell with Roxana K. Bell. -- 1st ed.
       p. cm.

    ISBN 0-89886-589-1 (paper)
    1. Cycling for children. I. Bell, Roxana K. II. Title.
    GV1057.2 .B45 1999
    796.6--dc21
                                   99-6062
                                   CIP

*To my brother John K. Bell,*
*my sister Shanna D. Bell,*
*my daughter Roxana K. Bell,*
*and to the memory of*
*my father R. Kenneth Bell,*
*with a toast to the great times*
*we have enjoyed together*
*bicycling and camping as both*
*kids and adults!*

# Contents

# Introduction

> "I want to take my eighteen-month-old son on my bike, but how can I possibly lug him, his diaper bag, and a picnic lunch?"

> "Our eight-year-old is shooting up like a beanstalk—but we just can't afford to keep buying him a new bike every other year. What about just getting him a big bike and letting him grow into it?"

> "Our five-year-old is visually handicapped. But I've heard that even blind kids can ride bikes. Is that true? How can I find out more?"

> "My twelve-year-old grew up in the city where no kid owns a bike. Now we're in the 'burbs where every kid rides. How can a kid that old learn to ride without feeling 'dumb'?"

> "Our eleven-year-old wants to race professionally. Where can he find out more about junior training programs?"

> "My fifteen-year-old nearly gave me heart failure the other night. I was driving home from work in the dark when, suddenly, two teenagers on one of those stupid clown bikes cut across directly in front of me from the opposing lane and kept on riding against traffic, weaving back and forth. Dark clothes, no helmets, no lights, the passenger with his legs stuck out. Then my headlights caught their faces—and I realized I'd nearly hit my own son. How can we stop this 'in-your-face—I'm-immortal' behavior before he gets killed?"

Real questions from real parents. That's what this book is designed to answer.

When I was blessed with my own daughter, Roxana, I wanted to share my lifelong love of cycling with her. But even though I'd been riding a bike for thirty-five years and had been writing about bicycling for nearly ten, the questions running through my mind made me realize I knew little more than any other first-time parent about how to introduce a child to bicycling.

I made plenty of mistakes as I figured out what to do (no one ever clued me in, for example, that a bike will fishtail alarmingly if a toddler is allowed to lie back in one of the reclining positions of a rear child seat). But I was also lucky: Roxana's mellow personality, long attention span, and enjoyment (when older) of being Mama's "test child" made her a good sport and valuable partner in learning.

Because I had acquired something of a local reputation as a commuting and touring cyclist, I was often buttonholed by other parents in my church, office, and neighborhood for information about family bicycling. Revealingly, they asked me the same questions I had been asking myself—how to ride with a baby, buy a child's first bike, get their children to wear helmets all the time (even when not around Mom or Dad), and teach youngsters how to ride in the street safely. They also complained about the flimsiness of department-store bikes. Some wondered where to get more information on learning to ride off-road trails or how to plan a tour for a group of kids. A few felt their own ignorance so keenly that they confessed they had essentially given up cycling when they became parents, not wanting to expose their child to cycling's danger.

In listening to them, it became clear that all of us shared a core of similar concerns, and each of us had a wide range of special concerns. That being true, why should every parent have to reinvent the wheel by trial and error?

The result is this book.

The tips and advice included here are drawn from my own experience with teaching novices about bicycle touring as well as from interviews with bicycle shop owners and mechanics, family cycling organizations, Effective Cycling instructors, manufacturers of child-oriented bicycling equipment, sports pediatricians, leaders of youth and Scout-troop rides, physical education instructors, and workers with special-needs children and teens. I also drew on the wisdom and experience of scores of parents who take their children out for bike trips long and short—and on the comments of kids themselves, who have clear ideas about how they do and do not like to learn.

Bicycling is a lovely way to grow together as a family. In addition to introducing children to a healthful, low-impact activity they can pursue into old age, bicycling can help them learn the value of regular exercise, good sportsmanship, and self-reliance. It can teach older kids defensive skills that will help them become more alert automobile drivers. Moreover, bicycling can be a wholesome and nonthreatening way for preteens and teens (and adults!) to meet friends and possibly dates.

Most important, of course, bicycling is fun—and a bicycle can literally be a vehicle for adventuring around the globe. You'll learn how in this book.

So, enjoy!

*Trudy E. Bell*

## A NOTE ABOUT SAFETY

Safety is an important concern in all outdoor activities. No book can alert you to every hazard or anticipate the limitations of every reader. The descriptions of techniques and procedures in this book are intended to provide general information. This is not a complete text on bicycling. Nothing substitutes for formal instruction, routine practice, and plenty of experience. Bicycling requires attention to traffic, road conditions, weather, terrain, the capabilities of the party, and other conditions. When you follow any of the procedures described here, you assume responsibility for your own safety.

*The Mountaineers*

# Chapter 1

# Bicycles and Accessories for Parents and Teens

As a parent, you're the linch-pin of the family team. From your child's birth through preschool at least, it is your bicycle that will support the weight of one or more children as well as yourself, a child carrier, and kid stuff—a combination that could top 250 pounds. It is your legs that will be the engine pedaling this load uphill and into the wind. It is your brakes that must be strong and reliable enough to stop all that weight at stop signs after a long downhill run.

For this reason, it is essential that you choose your bike and its accessories carefully, with close attention to safety, comfort, and reliability. Moreover, the information on desirable features and methods of fitting the bike to the rider given below are also applicable to any child tall enough—over about 5' 3"—to need an adult's bike.

## FEATURES OF A GOOD PARENT'S BICYCLE

Forget the advertising clutter touting racing bikes, cruisers, touring bikes, mountain bikes, BMX bikes, and all the rest. The rugged steed most parents buying a bike for the first time will like best is a cross, or hybrid, bicycle, so named because it combines features of a touring bike and a mountain bike.

A hybrid bike has a frame strong enough to carry heavy weight and a frame geometry that is stable under load—meaning that it will not shimmy (vibrate) when you and your child are coasting down a hill. It is also likely to have powerful, leveraged hand-operated brakes with large brake pads that will stop the bicycle effectively at the base of a downhill even if the wheel rims happen to be wet.

A hybrid's tires will be of a medium width ($1\frac{1}{4}$ to $1\frac{1}{2}$ inches) and of medium pressure (70 to 90 pounds per square inch)—neither as fat as the tires of a mountain bike nor as narrow as those of a road racer (see fig. 1-1). For hauling a child plus stuff, tires should be fat enough to support the weight and offer some shock-absorption over bumps,

*Figure 1-1. The medium-width tires of a hybrid or cross bicycle offer greater security under a child's weight than thin road tires but not as much rolling resistance as fat mountain-bike tires.*

*Figure 1-2. If your region is not flat, you will appreciate having a bicycle with a triple crank—a pedaling setup with three chainwheels that includes a powerful little alpine gear ("granny gear") for climbing hills.*

yet as narrow and high-pressure as practical so as to minimize rolling resistance on the pavement, which will make the bicycle less tiring to pedal.

Most important, a cross or hybrid bike has an adequate number of low gears, essential for pedaling your child's weight up even modest hills. Look for a bicycle with 18 or more speeds (gear ratios). Such a bike will be equipped with three chainwheels or front sprockets centered on the pedal cranks—a setup known in bicycle parlance as a "triple crank" (see fig. 1-2) and which includes a powerful little cog known as an alpine gear or "granny gear" (so named because with its leverage even your granny could climb hills).

You may be given a choice between drop or upright (straight) handlebars. This choice is a matter of personal taste. Drop bars allow you to bend forward in an aerodynamic tuck—useful for coasting down-hill or pedaling into a head wind. They also allow you to change the position of your hands, offering welcome relief on longer rides. Upright bars let the wind catch you full in the chest—but their greater width provides somewhat more leverage in controlling the bicycle under a child's weight, and sitting up higher gives you a better prospect of traf-fic or the scenery. *Tip:* If you opt for upright handlebars, ask about op-tional bar-end attachments that allow you to bend forward to ride in a more aerodynamic position when necessary.

## HOW TO MAKE SURE A BICYCLE FITS

Most full-sized adult bicycles, whether for a Mom (or adolescent) 5' 3" tall or a Dad 6' 7" tall, have a set of wheels that are one of three very similar standard sizes—designated as 26 inches, 650 C, or 700 C (the old 27-inch size is no longer used). Although the standard wheel sizes are similar in diameter (26 to about 26½ inches), frame sizes vary tremendously, both in height and in horizontal reach. Thus, you need to determine whether the bicycle frame fits you properly.

An adult's (or teen's) fit is determined by a balanced combination of three sets of measurements: vertical frame size (stand-over height), saddle position (leg extension, fore-aft placement, and tilt), and horizontal frame size (reach). Although avid cyclists debate the importance of additional measurements, getting these three basic ones right will minimize knee injury, deliver maximum power to the pedals, and ensure comfort.

The most important thing is to make sure that the bicycle's frame is not too big. A bicycle that is slightly too small is safer and preferable to one that is too large.

### Vertical Frame Size

For a bicycle with a horizontal top tube, determining the correct vertical frame size (stand-over height) is straightforward: when your feet (in flat-heeled shoes) are flat on the ground and positioned shoulder-width apart, there should be 1 to 3 inches of clearance between your crotch and the top tube (see fig. 1-3). For optimum handling of your child's weight, a larger frame (offering 1 inch of clearance) will be more stable than a smaller frame (offering 3 inches of clearance), assuming the other basic measurements are correct.

*Figure 1-3. Correct stand-over height (vertical frame size) for a road bike allows 1 inch between the horizontal top tube and your crotch. A mountain bike (not shown) should allow 3 inches.*

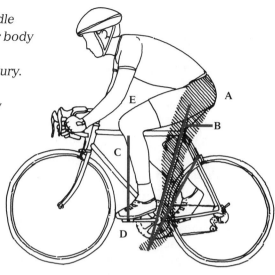

*Figure 1-4. Bicycle's saddle position needs to fit your body to maximize power and comfort and minimize injury. Saddle height (A) should allow the leg to be nearly straight—that is, have proper extension—at the bottom of the pedal stroke. When saddle is at the correct height, frame should be small enough to allow several inches of seat post to be exposed (B). Correct horizontal position of the saddle is determined by sitting on the bike and dropping a plumb line from the kneecap (C); saddle should be moved fore or aft on its rails until the plumb line intersects the spindle of the forward pedal when the crank arms are level (D). Reach (horizontal frame size) is correct for a bicycle with drop handlebars if your elbows are comfortably bent when your hands are on the drops around the brake levers (E).*

Determining vertical frame size is more difficult if the bicycle has a slanted top tube or a step-through frame, but an experienced bicycle mechanic at a pro bike shop can help. The frame sizes of many bicycles are specified by citing the distance in inches or centimeters from the center of the bottom bracket (that is, where the pedals attach to the frame) to the top of the seat tube. The proper size frame for you should be 10 to 12 inches shorter than the length of the inseam on a pair of well-fitting long pants worn with flat-heeled shoes.

### Saddle Position
The saddle is at the correct height when with your foot at the bottom of the pedal stroke your leg is nearly straight—knee only slightly flexed (see fig. 1-4). In that position, you will have what cyclists call proper leg extension, which is desirable because it maximizes power to the pedal stroke and minimizes stress on the knees.

With proper leg extension, your feet will not be able to touch the ground when you are seated on the saddle! A saddle set that low—commonly seen with novice riders—puts too much pressure on the knees while pedaling; a saddle set too high, however, causes the hips to rock back and forth while pedaling and puts too much pressure on the genitalia.

*Note:* With the saddle at the correct height, you should be able to wrap a fist around the projecting seat post. If obtaining proper leg extension requires you to shove the saddle all the way down in the seat tube, the bicycle's frame is too big; if the saddle has to be raised so high that you can see the warning line 3 inches from the end of the seat post, the frame is too small (for safety, at least 3 inches of seat post must remain inside the seat tube).

Once the saddle is positioned at the correct height, you can determine its correct fore-aft position, which will enable you to maximize force on the pedals. The saddle of a good-quality bicycle is on rails so it can be moved backward or forward by as much as 2 inches when the bolt at the top of the seat post is loosened (the saddles of low-quality bicycles can only be pivoted from a joint at the end of the seat post, and so this important fit adjustment cannot be made). Slide the saddle to the position where a plumb line suspended from the upper calf just below the knee would fall directly over the ball of the foot (and the pedal spindle) when the pedal is in the forward horizontal position.

*Note:* The saddle position for an adolescent should be checked once a month, as a growth spurt of an inch or two could significantly alter the necessary measurements.

Last, if necessary, tilt the saddle's nose just a smidge up or down. The greatest comfort will be obtained when the saddle's nose is level or tilted up or down just enough so that your weight is supported on your "sit bones" (the ischial tuberosities)—the two pelvic bones you can feel most prominently when you sit on a low step or curb. You don't want the nose pointed so far down that you keep sliding forward and resting most of your weight on your hands; at the same time, you don't want the nose tilted up so far that your weight is being supported by your soft genital tissues.

Women, with their wider pelvic structures, may prefer a saddle somewhat wider than men. But go for the narrowest saddle that is comfortable. A narrower saddle offers the least impediment and chafing to your legs while pedaling.

*Important:* Pain or numbness in the pubic or anal region during or after riding a bicycle is a signal that some fit or saddle adjustment needs to be made. In fact, it may take quite a few adjustments—even experimentation with optional padded seat covers or the many anatomically shaped saddle designs (including ones with a flexible nose, with a hole cut out of the nose, or with no nose at all)—before you happen on a combination that is most comfortable for you. A good bicycle mechanic will help patiently until you find nirvana. Don't give up.

### Horizontal Frame Size

Horizontal frame size (reach) is the length of the top tube plus the handlebar stem (the L-shaped gizmo that holds the handlebars in the steerer tube). Measuring reach is important because two bicycles having the same frame height may have top tubes whose lengths differ by well over an inch, depending on the manufacturer and frame geometry.

If the bike has drop handlebars, make sure that when you sit on the saddle with your hands relaxed on the drops around the brake levers, your elbows are comfortably bent (see fig. 1-4e). (Riding with straight arms will stress your neck and shoulders, causing muscle cramps, and may put pressure on the genital area that contacts the front of the saddle.)

For upright handlebars, use the "forearm test" to determine proper reach. Once the saddle is at its proper vertical and horizontal position, place your elbow at the saddle's nose and line up your forearm and outstretched fingers parallel to the top tube; the center of the handlebar should be no more than two finger-widths (about an inch) beyond the end of your outstretched hand.

If these tests indicate that the reach is too long, look at the horizontal part of the handlebar stem. If it's 2 or 3 inches long, then you can shorten the reach—move the handlebars back toward the saddle—by having a shorter stem installed. If the stem is already a stubby little guy and can't be shortened further, you should look either at the same size frame by a different manufacturer, or at the next size smaller frame.

## CARRYING KID STUFF ON A BICYCLE

Children—especially toddlers—can never be accused of traveling light. Everywhere a child goes, must go diapers or pull-ups, a spare outfit, diaper wipes and cream, a changing pad, bottles, an extra sweater—you know the drill. For a day trip, you may also want to carry a blanket and a picnic lunch. However can you carry all this stuff on a bicycle?

Never fear. All the racks and panniers (saddle bags) invented for touring cyclists and bicycle commuters serve parents exceedingly well, reverting to their original purpose when your child grows old enough to enjoy bicycle touring and camping.

Most rear racks bolt to the tops and bottoms of the seat stays that straddle the rear wheel. Rolled picnic or baby blankets can be

*Figure 1-5. Panniers on a rear rack can carry large items such as a baby blanket or diaper bag. Note seat post attachment for child's trailercycle.*

strapped onto the top of the rack, while diapers, bottles, and snacks can be slipped into panniers (see fig. 1-5) clipped onto the sides.

If your child is to be riding in a rear child seat, however, both the top and sides of the rear rack will be covered by the seat and its footwells and thus are not usable. In this case, you'll need a front rack for carrying all the child's goodies.

For the best handling, go with a low-rider front rack, which places the load low and symmetrically around the front wheel hubs (see fig. 1-6). You may even find that your bicycle is more stable with loaded low riders than it is with no load at all!

Panniers (pronounced "PAN-yers," rather than as the French might expect) are soft-sided saddle bags, usually with an internal frame, designed to clip onto the sides of a front or rear rack. They are typically made of heavy-duty Cordura, a tightly woven fabric similar to a light-weight canvas, which is coated on one side (the interior) to make it semi-waterproof. Panniers are designed to be hung and removed from a rack in two seconds with no tools. Sold in pairs, panniers often snap together for easy carrying off the bike.

Smaller panniers may be used interchangeably on front or rear racks (although the fastening mechanisms may have to be repositioned

Figure 1-6. Low-rider front rack (A) is stable for carrying smaller children's items; panniers attach to the sides (B).

for use on low riders). Larger ones are exclusively for use on the rear.

There are dozens of other types of bike bags, including handle-bar bags, rack trunks, duffels, wedges, fanny packs, messenger bags, and garment bags. Any good book on bicycle touring or bicycle commuting illustrates many of the designs with tips for their use. Such bags are sold at pro bicycle shops or through such reputable mail-order houses as Bike Nashbar or Performance (see Appendix 3, "Recommended Resources for Parents and Kids").

## IMPORTANT: GO FOR QUALITY

When you buy bicycles and bicycling-related equipment, you get what you pay for. For safety, durability, reliability, and enjoyment, go for the highest-quality equipment you can afford; quality will minimize mechanical mishaps (and thus expenses) and maximize the bike's performance (and thus your enjoyment of the experience).

The only place you can get a good-quality new bicycle—even for under $200—is at a pro bike shop. The markup on a bicycle in a pro bike shop is only about ten percent, while the markup on bicycles sold in toy or department stores is one hundred percent (pro shops make their money on accessories, not on bicycles themselves). Thus, a $200 bicycle from a pro shop represents about $180-worth of materials and labor; the components of an identically priced bike in a toy or department store are worth only half that amount. This difference translates directly into quality.

*Do not* buy a bicycle from a department store or toy store. You'll live to regret it—and to pay, literally, for the mistake.

A good-quality bicycle will balance well, its steel-alloy or aluminum-alloy frame is light-weight, and the low internal friction in its precision moving parts will make pedaling a breeze. It will brake to a secure stop and shift gears easily, and its hardened-steel parts will last years longer than those on a cheap look-alike. If stored indoors and given an annual spring check-up and lubrication, a high-quality bicycle will give you and your family riding pleasure for fifteen, twenty, twenty-five years or more.

A poor-quality bicycle may be unstable, and its carbon-steel frame is heavy. Its cheap bearings make pedaling a lot of work, and its brakes may not stop reliably. The wheel rims may be of such soft metal that spokes can't be tightened enough to make the wheels perfectly true (round and flat) without pulling the spoke nipples right through the rims. Even worse, the rims may be chrome, which becomes slippery when wet, dangerously reducing stopping power. Gear teeth, frame eyelets, and other parts may bend easily or break off under the weight of you and your child. Poor-quality bicycles commonly need repairs or adjustments every few months—which, if done in a shop, could well exceed the cost of the bicycle in a year. Moreover, you'll probably have to face replacing the bicycle altogether in two to five years.

At a toy store or department store, you have to accept the manufacturer's standard equipment. You may have to pay an extra $10 or $20 for the bicycle's assembly, which will likely be done by a stockroom clerk (unless you wish to put it together yourself). The sales clerk may also talk you into shelling out another $50 or $60 for a three-year "maintenance contract" that in fact offers very little that a pro shop might well do for free. There may be a maximum of a 30-day warranty for parts.

At a pro shop, however, the purchase price includes assembly, proper fitting of the bike to the proportions of your body, and a free safety check of all the components after thirty days of riding. Moreover, you may be able to specify various options (the type of handlebars, saddle, even gearing) just as you can for a new car; the only extra charge will be the differential—if any—in cost between what's stock equipment and what you prefer. The bicycle will be assembled by a professional bicycle mechanic, who knows that every screw must be greased before being inserted, knows not to bend spokes when inserting them into the rim, knows how to lace the spokes properly to give the wheels maximum strength, knows how to adjust the brakes to stop a squeal, knows just how tight is tight enough but not too tight for the headset and hubs, and knows not to put the handlebar stem in backwards . . . the list goes on. Also, a pro shop commonly offers a 5-year to lifetime warranty on the frame, and a 1-year warranty on parts and labor.

In short, a cheap bike is seldom really cheap.

*Money-saving tips:* First-quality machines at pro shops commonly sell for ten percent off in the late autumn and early winter during inventory clearance for the spring season. If you need to buy bicycles for two or more family members at once, you may also be able to negotiate a group discount. If you absolutely cannot afford the least expensive new pro-shop bicycle, consult the shop owner anyway: one of the mechanics or a local bicycle-club member may be selling a good-quality bicycle in good condition secondhand.

# Chapter 2

# Bringing Along Baby: Toddlers and Preschoolers as Passengers

Although some avid cyclists have been known to tow infants as young as a few weeks of age in child trailers, the American Academy of Pediatrics advises waiting until an infant's neck muscles are strong enough to support the weight of the head, and the child is strong enough to sit up unassisted. The Commonwealth of Massachusetts is more conservative, having actually made it against state law to carry a child younger than twelve months on a bicycle—a recommendation endorsed by the Bicycle Helmet Safety Institute.

Barring the existence of certain handicaps, you can count on safely introducing your offspring to a child trailer or rear child seat by around the time of the child's first birthday.

## CHILD TRAILERS

A child trailer is towed behind the bicycle, to which it is connected by a long hitch. In most designs, the hitch is attached to the left side of the bicycle's frame near the rear axle.

In some trailers the child rides facing the front, in others facing the rear. Some trailers are designed to carry two children weighing up to a total of 100 pounds (see fig. 2-1).

The child is secured into the trailer by straps that pass over both shoulders, across the lap, and up through the crotch. For the child's great-est comfort—especially if you would like to go on longer rides—make sure the trailer comes with cushions on the seat and back (preferably ones that can be removed for washing).

Larger trailers have plenty of room to carry a child's toys and snacks—and even sleeping bags or other gear for overnight trips. Many trailers can be fitted with netting or plastic to protect its young occupant(s) from wind, dust, rain, or cold—or from losing thrown bottles or toys.

Some good child trailers are hard-sided, others have fabric sides. Some may be folded so they will fit into the trunk of a car. Regardless of its material, make sure the trailer has a structural metal frame that completely encircles it (some cheap toy-store or department-store trailers are just one molded piece of plastic with a hitch bolted to the front). A metal roll cage should go over the child's head as protection should the trailer tip over (many toy store or depart-ment store models have no protection above the waist). The trailer's sides should be high enough to prevent little fingers from sneaking down and getting caught in the axle or the spokes of the

*Figure 2-1. A child trailer will fit one or two children from ages one to six.*

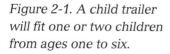

wheels (which are near the child's shoulders). Some models have a removable rear handle that allows the trailer to be pushed from behind, so it can double as a stroller—a great option on a multiday bicycle tour, or if you like to take your child(ren) along for a ride when you go out jogging.

For the best ride for both you and the child passenger(s), look for a trailer with 16-inch or 20-inch wheels, such as those that are standard on kids' bicycles. Large wheels will roll over small road defects instead of hanging up in them, as happens with wheels that are only 8 or 10 inches in diameter (smaller wheels are common in low-quality trailers). Inflatable tires will give the child a more cushioned ride than solid-rubber tires, which will transmit every vibration.

Look for wheels that are cambered—the axle is bent so that the tops of the wheels are an inch or two closer to the body of the trailer than the bottoms, like the wheels on manual wheelchairs. This design allows the trailer to be maneuvered through narrow spaces without hanging up on a projecting axle: if you can get the wheels through, you can get the whole trailer through.

Last, buy a trailer that is brightly colored for high visibility—yellow is great. Vertical flags placed at each rear corner are additional attention-getters.

### Safety Tips

Before taking your child out on the open road, take time to get acquainted with the new trailer's feel and tracking by towing it filled with 50 to 100 pounds of groceries, books, sand, or other inanimate weight.

Test to see if your bicycle's brakes are capable of stopping the extra weight at the end of a downhill run or in slightly damp conditions. Especially if your bicycle has only the side-pull brakes common on road bicycles or if you live in a hilly area, ask the bike shop to see about rigging up a third brake—one for the trailer's wheels—that is automatically activated whenever you squeeze the bicycle's brake levers.

You should also develop some technique for knowing without looking behind you just how close to the edge of the road you can ride before the trailer's right-hand wheel falls off the pavement onto the shoulder or into the gutter. This knowledge may turn out to be essential if you ever need to ride on a stretch of road with heavy traffic.

For example, Richard Mayberry, a bicycle mechanic in Kulpsville, Pennsylvania, discovered that when he is in his normal riding position, his child trailer's right wheel remains safely on the pavement so long as by glancing to his right he can line up his right brake hood with the white

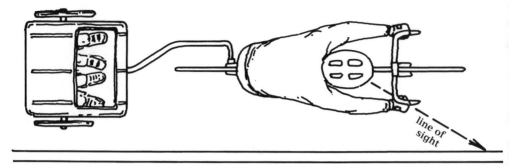

*Figure 2-2. Without looking back, this rider knows that his child trailer's right wheel will remain safely on the pavement as long as by glancing to the right from his normal riding position he can line up his right brake hood with the white line on the pavement's edge*

line at the pavement's edge (see fig. 2-2). Develop a similar mnemonic for yourself, using your own body height, handlebar proportions, and trailer width.

Mayberry cautions that you should never stand up to climb a hill with a child in a trailer, especially if the child is very young. Instead, stay seated and use your lowest gears. When you climb standing, the sideways rocking of your bicycle throws the trailer from side to side. If the movement is sharp enough, a very young child (twelve to eighteen months) might be frightened or even bruised. If the hill is so steep that you have no choice and must stand, keep the bicycle as upright as possible when you pedal.

## REAR-MOUNTED CHILD SEATS

A rear-mounted child seat allows a single child—usually weighing no more than 40 pounds—to be carried on a bicycle's rear rack. The maximum age represented by this weight limit varies widely with the build of the child. A child who is very tall or very heavy may outgrow a rear child seat by age three while a very petite child may be able to use it past age six; the average is probably around four or five.

The safest rear-mounted child seats (see fig. 2-3) have a back that comes up above the child's head (to prevent whiplash), sides that wrap forward (to protect the child's shoulders and arms in a fall), straps that come up between the child's legs and anchor over both shoulders

as well as across the lap (so the little body won't dangle and sway when snoozing), and straps for securing the feet in foot wells (so little toes don't get caught in the rear brake or spokes). Some rear-mounted child seats also have a padded grip bar that fits across the front at the child's elbow height to pillow the head if the child dozes off (see fig. 2-4).

Cheap child seats whose backs extend only up to the child's shoulders, have only a lap belt, or have no way of securing the feet are unsafe. Some low-quality child seats bolt permanently onto the back of the bike; if two parents want to share the toting of the child, they'll either have to buy two seats (one for each adult bicycle) or swap off riding the bike with the seat.

In contrast, good-quality child seats fasten onto the rear rack with quick-release locking devices and can be slipped off and on without much trouble (do watch your fingers to prevent their being pinched). Some models require a rack with a particular feature, such as a front section that rises from the flat surface vertically instead of at a 45-degree angle. *Hint:* If two parents will be trading off carrying the child, fit both bikes with the proper type of rack, which usually can be bought separately and is also useful for general carrying.

### Safety Tips

Even if the child seat can be reclined to allow the child to sleep, never use that feature. Always keep the seat (to use airline lingo) in its full and upright position. When the seat is reclined, the child's weight will be carried aft of your bicycle's rear axle, which will cause the bike to fishtail and degrade its handling. If the child dozes off, as happens on nearly every ride longer than an hour or so, simply let the little body slump forward against the shoulder straps—most children will still sleep soundly. But slow your pace and take bumps gently to minimize strain on the child's neck.

When your child is in the seat, do not rely on your kickstand alone to hold up the bicycle. The child's weight will likely cause the bicycle to rotate around the kickstand until it falls.

It is best to have another adult steady your bike while you lift the child into or out of the seat. If you are riding alone, however, loop a cable lock through your bike's frame and then lock the bicycle to a

*Figure 2-3. The safest rear child seats have a back that comes up above the child's head, sides that wrap forward, straps that come up between the child's legs and anchor over both shoulders as well as across the lap, and straps for securing the feet in foot wells.*

garage door handle, automobile door handle, tree, picnic table, bike rack, parking meter, or other sturdy waist-high object. Then lift the child into the seat, secure all straps, and steady the bicycle with your hip or knee before unlocking the cable lock. At your destination, roll the bicycle up against the object of choice, put down the kickstand, again steady the bicycle with your knee and hip, and lift the child out.

If you plus child, child seat, and kid stuff tip the scales at more than 200 pounds, you're putting a lot of stress on your bicycle's wheels, which can cause them to go out of true—especially the rear wheel, which bears most of the weight. Fathers in particular may find themselves breaking spokes and hauling their bikes to the shop every few months.

*Figure 2-4. As children often nap in rear child seats, adequate and safe restraints are needed.*

If your spokes keep breaking under you, consider riding a mountain bike (whose 26-inch wheels are just enough smaller than 700 C wheels to be more durable), or substituting a more durable 48-spoked 700 C rear wheel (standard 700 C wheels have 36 spokes) such as those used to support the weight of two riders on a tandem bicycle (bicycle built for two).

It is imperative when hauling so much weight that you keep the tires pumped up to the manufacturer's recommended specification. Also, to ensure adequate braking, make sure that when the brake levers are squeezed there is an inch of clearance between the brake levers and the handlebar grips (the lives of both you and your precious cargo are literally in your hands).

*Final note:* For safety, never exceed the specified weight limit for a child seat. And never try to strap two children into the seat.

## TRAILER VS. REAR CHILD SEAT: PROS, CONS, AND QUESTIONS

In bicycling circles, there is a heated debate as to the relative safety of a rear-mounted child seat versus a trailer. Little quantitative research has been done, and apparently nothing in the way of formal, controlled studies. But anecdotal information from experienced cyclists does highlight key differences.

A child in a rear-mounted child seat raises your center of gravity, which requires good upper-body strength, excellent reflexes, and experience for confident handling—especially if you're carrying a heavier child. If the bicycle should fall, the child will fall from a greater height than from a trailer—although a well-designed child seat, which wraps around the child's shoulders and comes up above the head, does offer some protection.

A child trailer has a low center of gravity, making for stable handling. Some cyclists claim it even makes a bicycle handle better than it does sans trailer. If the parent falls, the trailer may not even tip over—or does so only in a slow roll. Moreover, a good-quality trailer's roll cage and other superstructure surrounds the child for protection. Some trailers also have a suspension system that smooths out the ride for the child inside—particularly desirable if you plan long bicycle trips.

Trailers do have their drawbacks. A trailer including wheels can exceed 3 feet in width, compelling the parent to ride somewhat farther away from the right side of the road than he or she might normally choose, so as to keep the right-hand trailer tire on smooth pavement rather than in the gutter or on the shoulder. Even though the trailer may be brightly colored and heralded with waving flags, its width may cause some parents to fear that it is in danger of being clipped by cars passing too closely, especially on a narrow road. The longer wheelbase of a bicycle plus trailer also requires the parent to make wider turns. Cyclists who prefer trailers counter by noting that motorists usually give a trailer a wide berth, knowing that its occupant is a child.

A child seat is more compact and does not lengthen or widen the profile of the bicycle. A child seat is also much lighter than a trailer, weighing only a few pounds. Trailers—especially hard-shell models—can top 20 pounds even when empty, a factor that may be a deterrent in hilly areas.

A top-quality child seat costs half or even a third as much as a trailer. High-quality trailers approximate the price of a lower-cost bicycle—several hundred dollars. Over the life of the equipment, however, the cost per year may be the same, as a trailer can carry a much heavier child—possibly up to age six or seven (the child's head will probably bump against the top of the trailer cover before the child's weight exceeds the limit). And only a trailer will allow one parent to carry two children safely at the same time—which may be essential for larger families.

From the child's point of view, there will be qualitative differences. The trailer is very near the ground, which means that a forward-facing child's straight-ahead and upward view is of the bicycle's rear wheel, the rear rack (if any), and the riding parent's bum. This position may put the child in the way of splashes or grit thrown up from the rear wheel, especially if the trailer is open to the breeze. If the trailer is enclosed in plastic or mesh, however, the child's experience is predominantly the same as being inside a car (an advantage if you live in an area that is often chilly and damp, but a disadvantage in heat). In a trailer, the child is a good six feet back and down from the parent, so the parent cannot point out sights to the child and may have a harder time hearing the child whimper "I need to go potty!" A child facing rearward will not see the towing parent at all (although a second family member could ride behind to keep the child from feeling isolated).

From a child seat, the child will see the broad expanse of the parent's back, but will also have a higher vantage point for viewing all the horsies and cows. The parent can point out the sights, sing, or tell stories. The ride in a child seat may be slightly harsher, however, as the seat is directly above the bicycle's rear wheel and has no suspension.

In a trailer, there is plenty of room for books, toys, bottles, and snacks. In a child seat, any bottles or toys you wish to keep must be tied to the seat—on laces short enough so the objects do not get caught in the spokes of the rear wheel. Also, for better or worse, the child can reach right into your rear pockets—for bananas or raisins, but also for your sunglasses, wallet, or keys!

One distinct advantage of a trailer over a child seat, at least once your child is old enough to walk and climb, is that you need do little or no lifting—a boon for parents with bad backs. Once you hitch the trailer to your bike, your offspring can crawl into place, and once you clip the safety belts you're off. The only time lifting will be an issue is when you need to lift the trailer itself—say, into and out of a car trunk or van.

With a rear child seat, you will always need to lift your child in and out, but if the child is two or older this task can be eased if you ask the child to jump as you lift.

So, which setup is right for you—child seat or trailer? The best way to answer this question is to try both to see which you like best. A good pro bicycle shop will usually allow you to take test rides around a parking lot or even neighborhood streets. See how the motorists in your area respond to both setups and how secure you feel in traffic. See how much the handling of your bicycle is affected by the change in weight and center of gravity. See how easily each piece of equipment detaches from your bike and hitches to another or stows in your car. Consider how many children you have or are likely to have, and how big they are, and how close in age. Weigh all these factors in light of your budget and the likelihood of obtaining—and later selling—high-quality equipment secondhand. Then make your decision.

## BABY PASSENGER NO-NOS

There is a type of front-mounted child carrier, often seen advertised in airline-passenger mail-order catalogues (although rarely seen on the road), that consists of a seat that bolts onto the horizontal top tube of a bicycle. A child sits on the seat with the feet resting on folding pegs installed on the bicycle's down tube (the tube that extends from the steerer tube to the bottom bracket where the pedals attach).

Some parents love this arrangement. Your ability to balance is less impaired than it is with a rear child seat because the child's weight is centered over the bicycle frame instead of being over the rear axle. You can talk softly directly into the child's ear or hair. Feeling more of an active participant in the outing with a prime view of the scenery, the child is reportedly somewhat less likely to fall asleep than is usual on any ride longer than an hour in a trailer or rear seat.

The wind rushing past, however, will make the child feel colder than he or she would in a rear seat shielded by your body, so the child must be dressed in an adequate wind-breaking jacket even on a warm day. By the same token, you, who are doing all the physical work of pedaling do not have the benefit of the refreshing wind in the chest for cooling off, will feel hotter than you might riding the bike alone. A tall child may block your view, and it will be difficult for you to bend over into an aerodynamic tuck. The child is not strapped in, nor are the feet secured onto the pegs.

There are two reasons why this type of carrier is not recommended. Riding one-handed (as you will have to do if a child falls asleep in a front-mounted seat and has to be held in place) compromises your safety. Your balance is unstable with the child's dead weight on one arm, especially at stops; you cannot signal turns; and unless your bicycle has a coaster brake (operated by backpedaling your feet), you can operate only one hand brake. Of course, you could stop and let the child sleep in some grassy roadside spot, but stopping each time your pride and joy dozes off could put a crimp in any daylong or multiday bike tour; a child's nap time in a trailer or rear-mounted child seat, however, doesn't interrupt anything—you can just keep riding at your own pace with your own thoughts.

*Under no circumstances should you try to ride a bicycle while carrying a baby on your shoulders in a backpack-style infant carrier.* This arrangement is dangerously top-heavy: a six-to-nine-month-old baby commonly weighs more than 15 pounds, and a one-year-old 20 to 25 pounds. Even with upright handlebars, you will have to bend over to pedal, which will make the baby's head the highest point on the bicycle—close to six feet off the ground, if you are tall. Should you become overbalanced and fall, what will hit the ground the hardest will be your baby's head.

## EQUIPMENT: GO FOR QUALITY

Buy all child seats and trailers from a reputable pro bicycle shop. Never buy cheaper look-alikes from a department or toy store. You need high-quality equipment for several reasons.

First, for safety: Items classified as toys do not need to meet the same federal safety standards as items classified as bicycles or sporting equipment. Even manufacturers of high-quality play equipment may not have the necessary knowledge of the needs and physical stresses involved in bicycling to make safe equipment.

*Note:* The American Society for Testing and Materials (ASTM) has finished developing a child carrier seat standard, and is developing a standard for bicycle trailers. For maximum safety, look for child seats and trailers with ASTM certification.

Second, for durability: A high-quality bicycle trailer or child seat will be durable enough to last through several children.

Third, for enjoyment: High-quality equipment is lighter than cheaper look-alikes, meaning less work for you. It also offers better suspension and seat padding, meaning greater comfort and a smoother ride for your child—and thus no fussing at the prospect of a ride.

Last, high quality is an advantage for resale. According to Rick Politz, owner of two Pennsylvania bicycle shops, he usually has a waiting list of parents ready to pay up to seventy-five percent of the original purchase price for used equipment—especially trailers—in good condition.

## GETTING USED TO A CHILD PASSENGER

For parents unaccustomed to riding a bicycle carrying the extra weight of a child, the secret is: easy does it at first. Start with short, leisurely rides around the smooth, level, paved bike paths in a nearby family park. Try to choose times of the day when the paths are unlikely to be frequented by joggers, dog-walkers, little kids wobbling on their own bikes, or hordes of shouting bigger kids racing around.

The first thing you're likely to notice is that both getting the bicycle going and braking it to a stop take longer. Your balance may also feel different. Ride until you feel comfortable with the new handling.

In a few days, you may want to pack the bike into the car and drive to a more distant park or beach with a longer paved bike path. Try a 5-mile ride complete with picnic and nap under shade trees or splashing in a creek. Choose a path with a few gentle inclines to try out your bicycle's lower gears. You'll notice immediately that pedaling up even a modest slope—or on the flat into the wind—is good, honest work!

Fortunately, shifting gears on any derailleur bicycle sold since about 1990 is a no-brainer: all you have to do is rotate a shifter one click and you're in the next gear. Just remember: you need to keep pedaling whenever you shift.

You are in a good gear for hauling the weight of your child when your feet are going around *faster* than one complete revolution per second—that is, you have a cadence of 60 to 90 revolutions per minute. If your cadence is slower than that (a common mistake of novice cyclists), you are pushing too hard and will wear yourself out fast, not to mention risking injury to your knees. To achieve the proper cadence, find a gear that feels comfortable, and then downshift into one even easier. The spinning should feel almost effortless. (For more details, see "Advanced

Training: Teaching a Child How to Shift Gears" in Chapter 5).

After half an hour of practice on a paved bike path or in a parking lot, you will have figured out which "speeds" are lower (easier) and which are higher (harder). Don't worry if you think you aren't moving forward very fast. Just take your time and enjoy the ride—the tortoise will beat the hare every day of the week, simply by outlasting him.

Now you're ready to try taking your child for a ride around local streets with relatively light car traffic (hints for sharing the road with cars are given in Chapter 6). Don't overlook the fact that on fine days, you can use your bike for getting your child to and from the sitter, day-care center, or preschool—a nice way to squeeze a bit of relaxing exercise and family fun into the beginning and end of a work day—or for doing weekend errands.

As your traffic-handling reflexes and your bike-handling skills improve—and as your knees strengthen—you can begin to map out half-day or all-day bicycle outings for the entire family (some suggestions are given in Chapter 7).

## BICYCLE HELMETS

Beginning in 1987, individual states have been passing bicycle helmet laws for minors. About a third of the states (fifteen) now mandate bicycle helmets for all children below a certain age: Alabama, California, Connecticut, Delaware, Florida, Georgia, Maryland, Massachusetts, New Jersey, New York, Oregon, Pennsylvania, Rhode Island, Tennessee, and West Virginia. The age differs from one state to the next, ranging from under twelve to under eighteen (see Table 2-1), with some local jurisdictions having stricter requirements. Some states, such as Florida and New Jersey, levy fines for violations.

Although there are no statewide laws in Arizona, Illinois, Michigan, North Carolina, Ohio, Texas, Virginia, Washington, or Wisconsin, some local jurisdictions in these states have passed bicycle helmet ordinances, some of which pertain to cyclists of all ages, not just minors.

Some states have bicycle-helmet legislation pending. For the status of the law in your own state and locale, check with a local bicycle shop, police precinct, the state bicycle/pedestrian coordinator (see Appendix 4), or the department of transportation or motor vehicles. The status of helmet laws for minors in various states is compiled and updated by the Bicycle Helmet Safety Institute (see Appendix 3 for contact information).

Regardless of any legal requirement, you should equip the entire family with properly fitting, industry-tested bicycle helmets. And make sure parents and children alike wear them every time they mount a bicycle, no matter how short the ride or where it goes—even if it's just on the sidewalk in front of the house. All people on bicycles—including toddlers and preschoolers riding as bicycle passengers—should wear bicycle helmets as routinely as all automobile and airplane passengers wear seatbelts.

Table 2-1
MANDATORY STATE BICYCLE HELMET LAWS

| State | Ages | Effective Date |
|-------|------|----------------|
| Alabama | Under 16* | 1995 |
| California | Under 18* | 1994 |
| Connecticut | Under 15 | 1993/97 |
| Delaware | Under 16 | 1996 |
| Florida | Under 16#$ | 1997 |
| Georgia | Under 16 | 1993 |
| Maryland | Under 16* | 1995 |
| Massachusetts | Under 13+ | 1990/94 |
| New Jersey | Under 14$ | 1992 |
| New York | Under 14* | 1989/94 |
| Oregon | Under 16 | 1993 |
| Pennsylvania | Under 12 | 1991/95 |
| Rhode Island | Under 16 | 1996/98 |
| Tennessee | Under 12* | 1994 |
| West Virginia | Under 15 | 1996 |

\* Individual counties, cities, villages, parks, or other local jurisdictions have stricter laws than the state.
\# Helmet is required on public property only.
\+ Children under 12 months are prohibited from being passengers on bicycles.
$ Fines are assessed for violation.
Sources: Bicycle Helmet Safety Institute; individual state statutes

### What to Look For in a Preschooler's Helmet

Typically, bicycle helmets have an interior lining of crushable foam (which looks rather like dense Styrofoam) designed to absorb the force of an impact, surrounded by a thin outer shell of high-impact plastic. They fasten under the chin with clips, and the straps have adjustable fasteners. Helmets come with several sizes of softer foam fitting-sponges or pads that attach with hook-and-loop (Velcro) closures inside the foam shell to custom-alter the fit.

Helmets for toddlers and preschoolers are qualitatively different from those for older children or adults. The helmet encases the entire head, from forehead to the nape of the neck, and covers the ears, and it may not have ventilation holes. This is fine, because toddler passengers are not working up a sweat during the ride. Because small children often tend to feel colder than adults at any temperature and most body heat is lost from the head, a fully enclosed helmet will keep a small child comfortable even with the breeze rushing past. If your child is petite, a toddler helmet may fit as late as age six (although the lack of ventilation holes make it unsuitable for use by a child who is actively pedaling).

Do not buy a child an adult helmet and expect the child to "grow into it"—any more than you would buy a child adult-sized shoes. A helmet that is too big is unsafe. Also, do not buy an "aero"-shaped helmet for a toddler or preschooler: the helmet's projecting tail will bump against the back of the trailer or child seat and force the child's head to tilt downward, perhaps causing a stiff neck. If even a regular helmet does not allow the child to sit with the head in a natural position, place a pillow behind the child's back.

How do you know when the helmet fits properly? Leaving the chin strap unfastened, have the child bend over at the waist and touch forehead to knees. Does the helmet fall off or stay on? The helmet is properly snug when it stays on. If it falls off, it's too loose. You should insert the next larger size of fitting sponges and try again.

Once the helmet is properly snug, adjust the chin strap: the strap is tight enough if there is only enough room to insert one finger between the strap and the jaw (the child should be able to open the mouth comfortably).

All bicycle helmets manufactured after March 10, 1999, must by law meet a new standard put forth by the U.S. Consumer Product Safety Commission (CPSC). Helmets manufactured before March 10, 1999, can still be sold, however, and you might be able to find them at deeply discounted prices. For maximum safety, make sure any pre-CPSC helmet has a sticker inside noting that it meets or exceeds either the ASTM F1447 standard of the American Society for Testing and Materials or the B-90 or B-95 standards set by the Snell Memorial Foundation. Both the ASTM F1447 and the B-90 standards are similar to the CPSC standard, and the B-95 standard is more stringent. Avoid a helmet certified only to the old ANSI Z90.4 standard of the American National Standards Institute, as it will not adequately protect your child's head in a crash. And avoid any helmet having no certification sticker inside, as it is likely to have met no standard at all.

Unless the helmet carries CPSC, ASTM, or Snell certification (see fig. 2-5), do not buy a helmet at a toy store or department store—go to a pro bicycle shop. There's only one thing worse than no head protection for your child: putting your confidence in a product that you think will adequately protect your child's head—but will not.

## HOW TO GET A TODDLER TO WEAR A HELMET

Getting a toddler used to wearing a helmet while on a bicycle is akin to getting a child used to wearing shoes after spending the first year of his or her life barefoot. Most children resist the idea. But with the helmet you have a secret weapon: bicycles move and children love to go for a ride.

From the child's viewpoint—and perhaps even yours, if you have just started wearing a helmet as an adult to set a good example for your kids—the helmet feels weird. It encloses the head, feels a little heavy, and may alter the sounds of things a bit. The best approach to take is to encourage your toddler to a) tolerate it, b) forget about it, and c) like it, in that order.

Turn the first introduction of the helmet into a game. Don't tell the child to wear it because  you want him or her to, because every self-respecting independent-minded toddler will not want to for that very reason. Take advantage of the fact that toddlers love to play games of imitation and peekaboo. Hand your toddler the helmet and let him/her play with it—examine it, roll it around (a toddler shouldn't be able to hurt it). Eventually, if the child doesn't figure it out first, pop your own helmet onto your head, letting the straps dangle. Laugh!

*Figure 2-5. Look for stickers verifying that the helmet has passed the rigorous ASTM, CPSC, or Snell safety standards.*

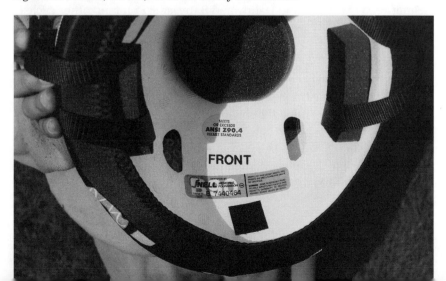

# Bicycling with Children

Guaranteed, your toddler will do the same with his/hers.

Take your helmet off, put it on again, several times. Then let your child take your helmet off your head and put it back on. Then it's your turn: take your child's helmet off and put it back onto his or her head—taking quick note as to how loose it is. While your baby is exploring your helmet, quickly insert some fitting sponges into the child's helmet. Resume the game, off, on, off, on—sneaking in fit adjustments, laughing, cooing.

When you think you have the fit approximately firm enough, encourage your toddler to look in the mirror with you. Put on your helmets, still leaving them unfastened, make faces, laugh at yourselves. Then bend over. Hopefully, the toddler will imitate you—and you can assess whether the helmet stays put or falls off.

Still in front of the mirror, fasten the chin straps. Many children will object to the feeling of something dangling or rubbing up under their chins. But use funny faces and other games of distraction, including a short game of chasing each other around the yard or room. The idea is to get the child to forget about this new thing on his/her head for at least a minute or two.

Now for the secret weapon! Lift the child into the bike seat or trailer and secure all belts. The novelty of this turn of events will be enough to distract the child until you are settled and ready to ride. Even better, as soon as the bicycle starts moving, the helmet and all else will be swept aside in the thrill of rolling forward, feeling the breeze, and watching objects and people speed by.

At first, your toddler may still fuss and try to push the helmet off, particularly when you must wait at stoplights. Talk soothingly or comically or point out the sights to provide distraction until the light turns green. Within a few weeks even this fussiness should stop.

Children older than two can begin to grasp the concept that a helmet keeps Mommy and Daddy and Baby safe. Point out other cyclists (especially children) wearing helmets. When you see cyclists who are not wearing helmets, ask your toddler "Is that good?" Begin to instill the idea that wearing the helmet is an essential part of the sport.

The key to success is to make absolutely no exceptions! No helmet, no ride—either for you or your child passenger. Not only does inconsistent use undermine the message of the helmet's necessity, it also introduces new sensations (such as the breeze ruffling the hair) that the child may come to prefer. Don't even admit the possibility.

You'll know you've carried the day for your family's safety when your children toddle up to you and request a bicycle ride—by handing you their helmets.

# Chapter 3

# Tandem Cycling: Parent-Child Teamwork

By the time your child is about four, he or she may be outgrowing a child seat or trailer, and you will need to consider either a trailercycle or a tandem bicycle (bicycle built for two).

A trailercycle may be rated to last your child up through about age eight or ten (65 to 100 pounds, depending on the model). A tandem bicycle will last all the way into adolescence and possibly adulthood, depending on how tall your child ultimately grows compared to you. Either option lets you keep riding as a family even though your child is not yet capable of bicycling in traffic or for any real distance.

With a trailercycle or tandem, bicycling with your child becomes a qualitatively different experience than carrying him or her in a child seat or trailer. The child is no longer a passenger but a second engine with separate pedals. The physical strength of little kids may surprise you—on flat ground even a preschooler can generate enough force to drive both you and your bike without your assistance for a short distance, and can put out a welcome burst of power to help crest a hill.

Tandem cycling is also a marvelous equalizer between riders of different abilities. The stronger rider can get a superb workout, the weaker one can go much farther or faster than would be possible alone, and the two are physically close enough to talk conversationally and share the experience. Thus, tandem cycling allows family bicycling even if a child has a visual, physical, or mental impairment (see Appendix 2, "Bicycling for Challenged Children").

## TRAILERCYCLES

A trailercycle is essentially the rear half of a child-sized bicycle that can be attached to any adult bicycle, turning your steed into an instant three-wheeled tandem (see fig. 3-1).

*Figure 3-1. Trailercycles (this one has a seat post attachment) turn an adult bicycle into an instant three-wheeled tandem. Note that for short parents, the curved attachment tube can collide with the rear reflector at the end of the rear rack.*

*Figure 3-2. Make sure the trailercycle has a chain from the pedals to its wheel, so the child can help pedal uphill instead of being just dead weight. This trailercycle also has a rear derailleur for low gears.*

A good trailercycle has pedals that drive a chain which propels its wheel (see fig. 3-2) so the child can help pedal up hills (some judicious bribery may be in order, though, as the trailercycle also has a freewheel, allowing the child to coast even if the parent is pedaling). Avoid cheap toy-store or department-store models that have no drive chain; it'll take only one hill with you pulling all 60-plus pounds of child and trailercycle for you to figure out why (a trailercycle alone commonly weighs about 20 pounds).

A good trailercycle comes with a handlebar and a seat whose positions can be adjusted to accommodate the child's growth. The better ones have a handlebar that slides along the top tube to increase both height and reach; cheaper ones have handlebars that just rotate while anchored in one location.

Trailercycles attach to the parent's bicycle via a special mechanism installed either on the seat post or the top of a custom heavy-duty rear rack. Higher-quality models have a quick-release mechanism that allows the trailercycle to be detached or attached in seconds—very handy if two parents spontaneously decide mid-ride to switch off who pulls the trailercycle. Avoid cheap models that require the entire attachment mechanism to be unscrewed and slipped off the seat post in order to detach the trailercycle from the bike—an unnecessary, time-consuming nuisance.

*Tip:* If you and another cyclist intend to trade off pulling the trailercycle, buy an extra attachment mechanism for the second adult's bike so that the switch-off is a matter of seconds. Also, if you share pick-up and drop-off duties while bicycle commuting to work, arrange to leave the trailercycle at the school with the child.

Look for a trailercycle that has standard 20- or (rarer) 24-inch wheels. Replacement 20- or 24-inch tires and inner tubes can readily be found in any bike shop around the country. Their 45 to 65 psi pressure and $1^1/_2$-inch width provide good support and not too much rolling resistance. Avoid cheaper trailercycles with 16-inch or 18-inch wheels. Although 16-inch wheels are a standard size, a trailercycle with such small wheels is unlikely to last your child to age ten. Small wheels may hang up in road defects slightly more often than larger wheels and may give a harsher ride. An 18-inch wheel is a nonstandard size and replacement tires and tubes are likely to be tough to find.

A rear derailleur and gear-shift lever that the child can operate is available as an option on high-end trailercycles. This is a nice feature if you anticipate having the child trailing behind you up to age nine or ten, and you hope to do multiday touring in which you will welcome the pedaling help on all kinds of terrain. Don't bother trying to teach a four-year-old how to shift gears, however, unless you want to hear the endless crunching of metal against metal in everlasting experimentation. In the case of younger children, tape the shift lever into place at the position of the lowest gear and be grateful if the little one helps pedal up a hill.

You'll likely pay a pricey premium for the capability to shift gears. But if you live in a hilly area, gears on a trailercycle may be worth the extra money if only because it will be possible to put the trailercycle in a low gear. The fixed gear of one-speed trailercycles, like that on one-speed bicycles, is the highest gear—the one hardest to use for climbing hills, and thus one that a child may balk at using.

Larger families may want to investigate trailercycles that have two or even three seats! It is also possible to hitch a child trailer onto the left rear axle of a trailercycle, so that a baby can also go along for the ride. To accommodate even more riders this arrangement can be pulled by a tandem to form a "bicycle train" (see fig. 3-3). (It is not possible, however, to hitch a trailercycle onto the back of a parent's bicycle that has a rear child seat, because the child seat blocks both the seat post and the top of the rear rack.) Cycling parents differ in their opinions about bicycle trains; some love them while others find the handling very unstable.

*Tip:* When you tow a trailercycle empty, the lack of weight allows the wheel to bounce, throwing off the chain so it drags on the pavement.

*Figure 3-3. Bicycle trains can keep even a large family riding together. Here, Richard and Karen Mayberry on their tandem tow son Joseph on the trailercycle and the author's daughter Roxana in the trailer.*

To prevent this, lift the chain off the chainwheel and drop it into the narrow groove between the chainwheel and the metal chainwheel guard where it will stay securely out of dirt's way. Just remember to put it back onto the chainwheel's teeth before your child rides again.

*Tips for short parents:* If you are under 5 feet 5 inches tall and have a bicycle with a rear rack, you may find that when your saddle is at the correct height, there is not enough clearance to fit the seat-post attachment mechanism onto the seat post and still clear the upward-projecting front of the rack. Consider instead the type of trailercycle that attaches to a mechanism on top of a custom rear rack. Alternatively, have a bike shop hacksaw off the rack's upward-projecting front end. Loss of this front end does not compromise the structural integrity of the rack—it just eliminates one place to which you can attach bungee cords. Just make sure the shop smooths off the hacksawed rods and paints them to match the rest of the rack.

Short riders may also find that the trailercycle's attachment tube, if it's of a curved design, bounces against the rear rack's end, shattering the rear reflector. This problem can be eliminated by buying a trailercycle whose front portion is not curved but extends straight back from the adult's bicycle and then bends downward only after clearing the rear rack. Alternatively, unscrew the rear reflector whenever the trailercycle is installed, and replace the reflector whenever the trailercycle is detached.

## Introducing Your Child to a Trailercycle

A good bike shop should allow you to bring in your own bicycle and test-ride several models of trailercycle in a nearby parking lot. Look primarily for stability of the ride for both you and your child. You might want to let your child participate in the purchase decision—perhaps by picking the color or even making a contribution from his or her allowance—so he/she will feel pride of ownership and look forward to riding this new addition.

If your preschooler or kindergartner has been riding for two to four years as a passenger strapped into a trailer or a child seat, the first ride on a trailercycle may make him or her feel insecure. He or she will be perched without a safety harness on a regular bicycle saddle that lacks a high back or sides and may fear falling off.

Reassure your child by pointing out that "if you keep your hands on the handlebars and your feet on the pedals, you'll do fine." Appeal to your child's memory of past experiences that were scary at first but later were found to be fun. Assure your child that, yes, he/she can do this, too—and that you, the parent, would not allow anything to hurt the child.

If possible, have a second adult walk along beside the child, with a comforting hand steadying the waist, talking soothingly. Stop the test ride when the child needs to regroup emotionally. Resume at your child's request, showing delight at such signs of growing confidence as asking to go a little faster. Correct your child for any overconfident, unsafe behavior (such as riding "no-hands"). Praise your child for taking a risk and trying something new, and talk about what fun times you will have together.

## A BICYCLE BUILT FOR TWO

A tandem bicycle accommodates parent and child (or two adults) on one two-wheeled, extra-long bicycle frame (see fig. 3-4). The tandem has two saddles, two handlebars, and two sets of pedals. Because the bicycle is carrying the weight of two people, certain parts of it are larger and stronger than is typical on a standard single-passenger bicycle. Tandem wheels, for example, typically have 48 spokes instead of 36, and the frame's headset is fatter. There may be an auxiliary third drum, disk, or hydraulic brake, which is especially helpful for families who may wish to plan tours in regions with long or steep downhills. A typical tandem weighs 40 to 45 pounds, more than the average single bicycle, although less than two.

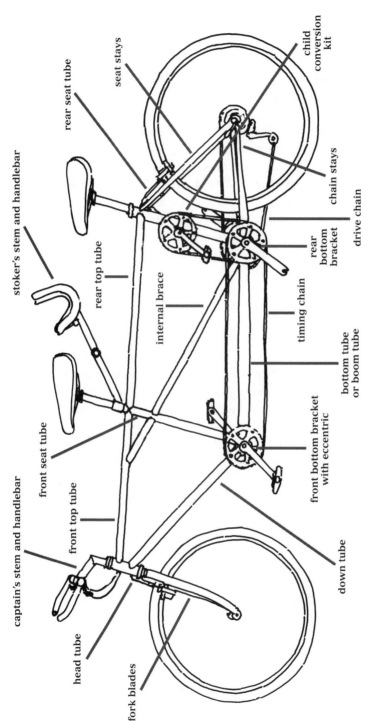

Figure 3-4. The principal parts of a tandem are shown in this diagram. The frame design shown is a variant of the direct lateral, which is the most common one found on stock tandems, and which will accommodate a conversion kit for a child to ride stoker (that is, on the rear saddle).

The rider in front is known as the captain (or pilot); the rider in back is known as the stoker; child stokers are colloquially dubbed "stokids." Usually the captain is the more experienced cyclist—the parent in a parent-child pair. The captain is responsible for steering, braking, shifting, and pedaling. The stoker is responsible for pedaling, and for having a good time. (Older kids riding as stokers can also be made responsible for navigating from the map, taking photos, obtaining necessary items from the captain's jersey pockets, and similar duties.)

Because tandems are specialty items, not every bike shop sells them. You'll probably have to go to a large specialty pro shop (most large metropolitan areas probably have one or two; look in the Yellow Pages or check the various bicycling magazines and see if the display ads specify tandems). For more information on tandem cycling, see Appendix 3, "Recommended Resources for Parents and Kids."

### *Childback Conversion Kits*

Because tandems with standard 26-inch or 700 C wheels are sized for the captain's stand-over height, the bicycle will be far too large for a child stoker. This can be remedied. Childback conversion kits (also called "kidback" kits), which consist of an extra bottom bracket assembly with chainwheel, chain, pedal cranks, and pedals, are readily available (see fig. 3-5). The kit is bolted onto the stoker's seat tube, with the extra chain running from the kidback's chainwheel down to the tandem's front or rear chainwheel, so the child can contribute to the pedaling. The kidback should be set low enough so the child's leg is properly extended at the bottom of the pedal stroke when the saddle and handlebars are adjusted to be comfortable for the child.

Most kidback kits require the "stokid's" feet to keep turning at the same cadence as the captain, even if the child is just resting and not exerting any pedaling force. Many cyclists feel this is excellent training in proper pedaling technique for an older child, but it could be too demanding for a younger one. For that reason, although children as young as two and a half have ridden as "stokids," four or five is a much more common starting age. (If desired, it is possible to get a kidback with a freewheel, so the child can pedal or coast as desired, just as on a trailercycle.)

For safety, it's a good idea to replace a kidback's ATB pedals, which have sharp gripper edges, with smooth plastic pedals and to install toe clips to secure the child's feet. Both precautions will prevent the child's shins from being barked if his/her feet should slip off the pedals while the captain is pedaling. Also, make sure the child's shoelaces

Figure 3-5. Childback conversion kits allow even a very young child to help pedal a tandem bicycle. Note how little Joe Mayberry has proper leg extension at the bottom of the pedal stroke, just like his dad, Richard.

are double knotted and tucked into the shoes to keep them away from shoelace-eating chains.

The captain, whose seat tube is suspended midway down the frame, will have a very smooth ride on a tandem—but because the stoker's saddle is almost directly over the rear wheel, the ride in that position is rougher. For the child's comfort, install a padded seat cover (gel or fleece) on the rear saddle and make sure your little one has padded bike shorts (see "Necessary Accessories for 'Stokids'" at the end of this chapter). For a heavier child, or for multiday trips, you may want to consider installing some kind of suspended seat post (if the stoker ain't happy, ain't nobody happy).

Note: There are at least a dozen different frame designs for tandem bicycles. Childback conversion kits may not fit on tandems on which a bracing tube intersects the top or middle of the stoker's rear seat tube—notably the uptube and marathon designs. Before purchasing any tandem, check this out with the bike shop owner. Fortunately, the most common tandem frame design, known as the direct lateral—which has a bracing tube running from the head tube to the rear bottom bracket (see fig. 3-4)—will accept a kidback.

# Bicycling with Children

One company has introduced a 21-speed tandem bicycle specifically designed for families. It has 20-inch wheels, which allow even a first-grader to stand astride the frame. Telescoping seat tubes allow quick adjustment for captains ranging in height from 5' to 6'5" and for stokers from 36" to 6'2". Thus, both Mom and Dad could switch off riding with the stokid or the parents can even ride together (see fig. 3-6). Another company has introduced a child's tandem with 20-inch wheels that will fit a captain as young as seven years old (see Appendix 3).

*Figure 3-6. Family Tandem by ATB Greengear of Eugene, Oregon, can be quickly adjusted to accommodate captains from 5' to 6'5" and stokers from 36" to 6'2".*

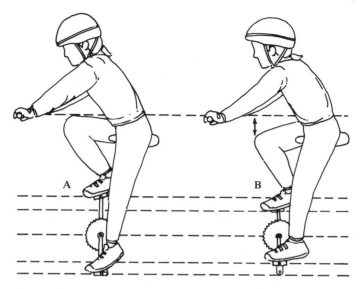

*Figure 3-7. Top: Pedal-crank arms that are too long (A) will cause a child's leg to be hyperflexed (bent too sharply) at the top of the pedal stroke and create too long of a leg extension at the bottom. When the pedals are repositioned with a crank-arm shortener (B), the child can spin at adult cadences without hyperflexure of the knees or rocking of the hips.*

## Shortening Pedal Cranks for "Stokids"

The pedal-crank arms on a childback conversion kit may need to be shortened to reduce the diameter of the circle made by the feet while pedaling. According to bicycle-shop owner Larry Black, crank-arm length is the critical measurement to be considered when bicycling with children.

With too long a crank arm, the child's knee will be hyperflexed—bent up to the chest—at the top of each pedal stroke when the child has proper leg extension at the bottom (see fig. 3-7). Hyperflexure risks injury to the child's knee joint and causes the child to rock the hips on the saddle while pedaling—reducing pedal power and making pedaling at adult cadences uncomfortable and difficult.

According to Black, the length of the pedal-crank arm, measured in millimeters, should be no more than ten percent of a child's height. Thus a child 39 inches tall (or about 975 mm, figured at 25 mm per inch) should use a crank arm no longer than 100 mm. Standard pedal-crank arms are 150 to 165 mm long, while childback setups typically have cranks around 110 mm long. Unfortunately, shorter crank arms are expensive custom items.

An inexpensive solution is to bolt a crank-arm shortener into each too-long crank arm. The crank-arm shortener is a piece of metal perforated with three or four threaded holes that allows the pedal to be screwed into the crank arm closer to the spindle, effectively reducing the length of a standard crank arm to 100 or even 90 mm. As the child grows, the pedal can be moved to the next hole away from the spindle (see fig. 3-8).

Crank-arm shorteners might also be advisable on the child's own bicycle as well. They also can increase the comfort and decrease the knee stress of parents who are under 5 feet tall.

## TRAILERCYCLES VS. TANDEMS: PROS AND CONS

The trade-offs between trailercycles and tandems are principally matters of short-term versus long-term cost and of handling on the road.

How long a trailercycle may serve your family will depend on the size of your children. If your kids are petite and slight, you'll get more years of use out of a trailercycle than if they are tall or heavy. Your kids won't outgrow the stoker's seat of a tandem bicycle, however, until they grow taller than the captain parent.

Once the trailercycle has been outgrown by the last child, there is no other earthly use for it (short of storing it while awaiting grandchildren!). A tandem bicycle, however, can continue to be ridden by the parents themselves, well after the last child has left home. A tandem bicycle is also the better long-term investment if a child is handicapped or disabled and will likely continue to bicycle with the parents after attaining adulthood.

### Trade-offs in Handling

A trailercycle that attaches to the seat post alters the handling of an adult's bicycle—something more noticeable to a lighter-weight rider on a thin-tire drop-handlebar road bike than to a heavier rider on a fat-tire bike with upright handlebars. Kids pedal unevenly. With a burst of enthusiasm, they'll carry you both, and then fall back wailing, "I'm tired!" If your tailgunner decides to lay on a burst of power, his or her pushing heavily on the pedals on alternate sides of the trailercycle will cause your bike to lean quickly back and forth; such leaning torques your steering, and requires some upper-body strength and agility to correct. This skittishness is somewhat less in trailercycle models that attach to a mechanism anchored to a rear rack above the adult bicycle's rear wheel.

A childback conversion kit on a tandem is "by far the best, most stable setup for an adult and child riding team," noted Stephen M.

*Figure 3-8. Crank-arm shorteners shorten the effective length of standard pedal-crank arms for a child, and also can accommodate the child's growth.*

Ciccarelli, the owner of a bicycle shop in Falls Church, Virginia, in a message posted on the Internet on the "touring@cyclery.com" listserve on January 8, 1997. "The two are within earshot and reach of each other, allowing the adult to hand water to the child and the child to access the jersey pockets of the adult." In his opinion, the linked pedaling is also a plus. "When Scott (six years old) decides he's tired on the [trailercycle], he's dead weight. On the tandem he can let up and even apply no pressure at all to the pedals, but he's still required to make his legs go around, thus learning the fundamentals of bike handling, etc. This will serve him well when he grows and we ride tandem a bit more seriously (if he chooses to). Likewise, with its third wheel, the trailercycle tracks differently than the primary vehicle, so leaning feels 'different.'"

Regardless of whether it attaches to the seat post or the top of the rear rack, using a trailercycle precludes carrying stuff on the top of the rack. You may still, however, be able to clip rear panniers to the sides of the rack. On a tandem bicycle, both the top and sides of a standard rear rack can be used.

### Trade-offs in Cost

Ultimately, the determining factor for any family may be the family budget. The cost of a trailercycle is comparable to that of a child trailer or an entry-level adult bicycle from a pro shop—that is, a few hundred dollars (additional seats and gears drive up the price). As with trailers, the resale value of high-quality trailercycles through bicycling channels (shops, clubs, swap meets) is high—and through those same channels, you may also be able to find a used model for somewhat less money than you would pay new.

Trailercycles are far cheaper than tandem bicycles. An entry-level trailercycle costs about the same as just the childback conversion kit for a tandem. Decent tandem bicycles range from around $1,000 to $6,000.

But those on a budget should take heart: anticipating a major expense can make it more affordable. If you set aside as little as $5 a week beginning in your baby's infancy, by the time the child is four you will have accumulated more than $1,000, exclusive of any interest earned.

## COMMUNICATION IS VITAL

While you are riding with a child on either a trailercycle or tandem, it is imperative that you keep up verbal coaching and communication. This need was made clear to me in a terrifying way. Shortly after buying a trailercycle, I rode with four-year-old Roxana up to a red light and put my foot down to steady us both. When the light turned green, I simply pulled ahead, just as I would have done with her in the child seat. Instantly, the back end of my bike wiggled and felt suddenly light, and I heard a loud wail; I stopped to see that Roxana had tumbled off the trailercycle and was sitting in the gutter, crying.

White at the thought of what would have happened had an automobile been behind us making a right turn, I pulled Roxana and the bicycle-and-a-half onto the sidewalk. After hugging and calming her, I asked her what had happened. The story emerged that when we had pulled up to the red light, she had also taken her foot off her pedal and put it down onto the pavement. "But why did you do that?" I asked. "I can hold up the bicycle for both of us."

"But I want to do what you do, Mama," she wailed.

Out of the mouths of babes comes the greatest wisdom. Use a child's desire to do what you do to inculcate good habits, such as wearing a helmet and following traffic laws. But be aware that having trained a child to imitate your actions, when you want the youngster to do something *different* from what you do, then you must explain what is needed and why, and reinforce that with repeated verbal coaching.

After that horrible moment, Roxana and I began every twosome ride with the trailercycle with a little ritual. I would sing out: "What are the rules?"

And she would reply: "Keep your hands on the handlebar, your feet on the pedals, and your bottom on the seat!"

Whenever we'd come up to a traffic light, I would remind her: "Even though I'm putting my foot down, keep your feet on your pedals." And when I saw the light was about to turn green, I would check on her in my helmet-mounted rearview mirror and warn: "Okay, are your feet on the pedals? We're about to go!" Likewise, on a tandem bicycle, the stoker should keep his or her feet secured on the pedals at stops.

Communication is necessary even before you begin moving. Mounting either a bicycle-trailercycle pair or a tandem bicycle requires a bit of practice. First, make sure that you and your child have helmets snapped and other equipment secured. Then coach your child: "Wait while I get onto the bike." Swing your leg over the top tube and hold the bicycle steady. "Okay, you may get on!" The child then should mount the trailercycle or kidback. Once on the kidback, the child should cinch the toe clips over his or her feet by pulling on the straps. If you're on a trailercycle, ask: "What are the rules?" After hearing the recitation about hands, feet, and seat, ask: "Are you ready to roll?" Make sure you get a solid affirmative answer before you move (you don't want the child to be unbalanced by, say, bending over to scratch an itch on a lower leg).

On either a trailercycle or a tandem, the captain is responsible for warning the stoker of any upcoming bump, so the stoker can lift a little from the saddle. Remember, the ride is harsher in the back, and a bump for which one is unprepared can be as jarring as an unexpected extra stair step. On a tandem bicycle, the captain should also warn the stoker of upcoming downshifts (so the stoker can push less hard on the pedals), as well as turns or stops (so the stoker can be braced for the change).

If the "stokid"gets sleepy (you may feel the telltale bump of a helmet against your back, or feel that things are mighty silent behind you), the captain should pull over and stop as soon as possible. You don't want the child to tumble from the saddle into the road—and besides, a communal nap on the grass can be mighty pleasant!

## NECESSARY ACCESSORIES FOR "STOKIDS"

For the child's feet, comfortable walking shoes are the best choice and have the added benefit of leaving him or her prepared for a spontaneous hike along a nearby trail. Sneakers are adequate—just make sure the shoelaces are double knotted and short enough not to get caught in the chainwheels. Do not let a child bicycle in sandals or bare feet; there is at least one case of a cyclist having a toenail ripped off when riding in sandals.

Once a child graduates to a trailercycle or tandem, the effort of pedaling will heat up the little body and generate perspiration, just as it does with Mom or Dad. Moreover, the child's hands are exposed to the same road shock and risk of falling as yours, and the pelvic bones are subject to the same vibration and the legs to the same chafing of the saddle.

Especially if you plan to be taking rides of longer than 5 miles, celebrate the child's new status by going back to the bike shop and investing in four "graduation gifts": a ventilated helmet, fingerless padded bicycling gloves (see fig. 3-9), padded bike shorts, and a bright yellow cycling jersey.

A helmet for a pedaling child needs more ventilation than that worn by a child passenger (for a discussion of helmets for school-aged children, see Chapter 4).

Fingerless padded bicycling gloves fill the role of helmets for the hands. Not only will they protect the child's palms in the event of a fall, but they will lessen road shock on hands and arms (including delicate tendons and nerves).

Padded cycling shorts protect the pelvic "sit bones" from bruis-

*Figure 3-9. A tandem-cycling or independently riding child should be equipped with padded fingerless cycling gloves to cushion against road shock and falls.*

ing road shock—these are especially important if the child is bony or heavy, and/or you anticipate taking rides longer than 5 or 10 miles. The best padding is either genuine or artificial chamois (an insert of polypropylene may keep the skin dry but is pretty useless as cushioning). Cycling shorts are generally longer than ordinary shorts in order to prevent the inner thigh from chafing against the nose of the saddle; they also have elastic hems that hold them in place and prevent the thighs from chafing against the inseam of the shorts themselves. Black is the standard color, as it doesn't show the places where a child (or adult) wipes off the chain grease!

Some pro shops and mail-order houses sell bike shorts specifically for kids—but extra-small adult sizes will work if your child is not toothpick-thin. If more padding is needed, you can cover the saddle with a gel or fleecy wool seat cover (gel is more durable).

A cycling jersey of high-visibility yellow is important since your pride and joy is now bringing up the rear (see Chapters 6 and 8 for more information on being visible to motorists). Cycling jerseys are made of polypropylene or light wool that wicks moisture away from the body and are thus superior to cotton T-shirts. When clammy with sweat, cotton can chill a child at stops on a cool day; in addition, cotton can become abrasive when damp and can rub the skin raw at friction points (such as under the arms). Cycling jerseys have pockets at the small of the back, where pedaling thighs won't keep hitting items carried in them. Often they also have elastic around the bottom hem so they won't ride up and flap around the shoulders on long downhills or catch on the nose of the saddle (as do oversized T-shirts). *Fashion tip:* Many tandem cycling pairs like to wear matching outfits!

# Chapter 4

# Buying and Caring for Children's Bicycles

The two key secrets on how not to go broke buying children's bicycles are: buy quality and insist that children take proper care of their bikes. If you're really budget-minded: buy quality secondhand.

## BICYCLES FOR THE AGES

Unlike adults' bicycles, children's bicycles are sized by their wheels. Standard wheel diameters for children's bicycles are 12, 16, 20, and 24 inches.

Depending on the build of the child, bicycles with 12-inch wheels generally fit two-and-a-half- to four-year-olds, while bicycles with 16-inch wheels generally fit four- to seven-year-olds. These smaller single-speed bicycles come standard with training wheels, a kickstand,

*Figure 4-1. A 16-inch bicycle generally fits children aged four to seven. The child should be able to stand astride the frame when feet are flat on the ground.*

and coaster brakes (see fig. 4-1). With their slanted top tubes, padded tubing, padded handlebars, and fat tires, they are designed to look like BMX bicycles—the small-framed agile stunt bicycles used for BMX (bicycle motocross) racing and freestyling (for more about BMX activities, see Appendix 1, "For Kids Only: Bicycling for Fun and Profit").

Bicycles with 20-inch wheels generally fit seven- to ten-year-olds. Training wheels are no longer standard equipment. Although they may look a bit like BMX bicycles, high-quality 20-inch bicycles can be legitimate riding machines. Many still have coaster brakes, but some are equipped with short-reach front and rear hand cantilever brakes—which are far superior for stopping at higher speeds. Kickstands are still standard. Some 20-inch bikes have a rear derailleur offering six or seven speeds (gear ratios)—a boon that frees you to take your child riding in places that are not pancake-flat (see fig. 4-2). *Note:* the 2-inch knobby tires that are standard on 20-inch mountain bikes will be tiring for a child to ride on a long road tour, but they can be replaced by 20-inch smooth road tires, readily available at many bike shops.

Bicycles with 24-inch wheels are essentially petite versions of adult bicycles; depending on the size of the child, they may fit children from age nine to the early teens, and can also fit adults shorter than about 5 feet 2 inches (see fig. 4-3). With a bit of searching through bicycle shops and reputable mail-order houses, it is possible to find genuine road racers and touring bikes with drop handlebars and narrower wheels, as well as hybrids and mountain bikes with upright handlebars and knobby tires in the 24-inch size. Just like full-sized adult bikes, high-quality 24-inch bikes come with hand brakes, as well as with front and rear derailleurs offering a full complement of gears—including a granny gear, which is valuable for climbing really steep hills. Neither kickstands nor padding on the tubing is standard.

Standard adult bicycles with 26-inch, 650 C, or 700 C wheels will fit any child who is at least 5 feet 3 inches tall. Since their wheel sizes are so similar, the sizing of adult bicycles is specified by the length of the frame's seat tube (see Chapter 1, "Bicycles and Accessories for Parents

*Figure 4-2. A 20-inch bicycle generally fits children aged seven to ten. Some, like this one, are genuine mountain bikes, complete with gears (rear derailleur) and hand brakes.*

Figure 4-3. A 24-inch bicycle generally fits children aged nine to fourteen, as well as some small adults. The features of these bikes are very similar to full-sized adult bikes (rear wheel of full-sized bike is shown for comparison); on this road-racing bike, note drop handlebars and triple crank.

and Teens") instead of by wheel diameter. Because they do not reach their mature height until late in adolescence, boys who graduate to an adult-sized bicycle by age twelve or thirteen may need another bicycle with a larger frame before they leave high school.

Aside from paint color and decorations, there is no longer a distinction made between "girls'" and "boys'" bicycles for any age. All 12-, 16-, and 20-inch bicycles have identical slanted top tubes and padding. In the 24-inch and larger adult sizes, a few models may have a step-through frame—that is, a frame whose top tube is set low to allow cycling in a skirt—but the choice of models is limited. The old-style "girls'" V-frame with no top tube has long been discontinued because of the inherent structural weakness of the open side; it is now standard for girls and women to ride the structurally stronger diamond frame (what used to be called the "boys'" or "men's" frame) with its horizontal top tube.

## CHOOSING A SMALL CHILD'S BICYCLE

*Even for a toddler, buy a true chain-driven bicycle with coaster brakes.* Make sure that the pedals of this tiny, first-ever 12-inch bike drive a chain to the rear wheel, just as they do on an adult bike.

The rear wheel of a chain-driven child's bike will come equipped with a coaster brake. A child riding down a hill simply lets the feet rest on the stationary pedals and coasts. To stop, the child backpedals half a revolution until the feet encounter resistance; then the child pushes down until the bike comes to a halt.

Do *not* buy the style of toddler bike—commonly found in department stores or toy stores—on which the pedals attach directly to the hub of the front wheel as they do on a tricycle (see fig. 4-4). Such direct-drive bikes have three drawbacks. First, the rider's legs must be longer to reach all the way forward on all parts of the pedal stroke than they need to be with a chain-driven bike of the same size, delaying the age at which a child may ride it. Second, with a direct-drive bike, as with a tricycle, each push on the pedals throws off the child's steering, first to the left and then to the right. A preschooler's steering will be unstable enough without that added destabilizing force.

Third, and most important, a direct-drive bicycle does not coast and has no brake, any more than does a tricycle. In theory, a child heading down a hill can slow the bike by exerting backward force on the always-rotating pedals. In practice, that requires more strength, coordination, and presence of mind than most small children possess. What happens can be very dangerous, even on a gently sloped driveway: as the pedals start turning faster, the child can't keep up and lifts his or her feet off them altogether. Now the spinning pedals will knock away the feet and prevent any attempt to regain control. At best, the child steers toward grass or dirt (which provide some friction to help slow the wheels) or heads uphill (gravity will bring the bike to a halt), or begins dragging the feet (which could get caught beneath the rear wheel). At worst, the child stops only by falling or by crashing into something—risking both injury and loss of self-confidence. In short, a direct-drive bicycle is horribly unsafe.

### Fitting a Child's Bicycle

For safety and comfort, the bicycle must fit your child's body. Do not buy a bicycle that is too big for your little one, reasoning that he or she will "grow into it." **A bicycle that is too large is a bicycle that is unsafe,** both because a bike that is too big for its rider is hard to control and because of the risk of injury (such as bruising the crotch area on the top tube).

*Figure 4-4. This direct-drive toy bicycle has no brakes, and pedaling throws off its steering; its two-and-a-half-year-old rider would be safer on a proper 12-inch chain-driven bicycle with coaster brakes.*

Since young children grow so quickly, however, the measurements used are a bit different for smaller children than for older kids, teens, and adults.

For children just learning to ride, the bicycle should be small enough that when the saddle is pushed all the way down to the frame, the balls of the child's feet can rest on the ground.

For confident riders, reaching the ground from the saddle is unimportant; instead, check for proper leg extension (see fig. 5-6). First, make sure the saddle can be raised high enough so that the child's leg is nearly straight at the bottom of the pedal stroke. With the saddle at the correct height, make sure there is a good 5 or 6 inches of seat post still inside the seat tube, so the saddle can be raised farther as the child grows.

For all children, there should be at least an inch of clearance between the child's crotch and the top tube when the child is standing flat-footed astride the frame (see figs. 4-1 and 1-3).

The final measurement involves reach: when the child is seated on the properly raised saddle with hands on the handlebar grips, the elbows should be a bit bent—enough so that when the child turns the handlebars, both grips remain securely within reach.

How can you tell that your child has outgrown the current bicycle? It's time for the next size when the child's legs have a pronounced bend at the bottom of the pedal stroke—that is, the child no longer can attain proper leg extension—even when the saddle has been raised up to the warning line on the seat post (see fig. 4-5). (Never raise the saddle

Figure 4-5. If the child's legs are bent when at the bottom of the pedal stroke, and the seat post cannot be raised any farther without exposing the limit line, the child has outgrown the bicycle and needs the next size larger.

higher than the warning line on the seat post; for safety, at least 2 or 3 inches of seat post must remain inside the seat tube.)

When the child is big enough for a 20-inch bicycle, you should add a new fitting measurement: each time you need to raise the saddle to accommodate the child's growth, also check the horizontal saddle position. As with an adult, correct horizontal saddle position ensures that pedaling puts the minimum strain on the child's knee joints while putting maximum power to the pedals. Since a child on a 20-inch bicycle may be big and strong enough to be riding 5 to 35 miles in a day (yes, indeed), such considerations are important.

The saddle of a good-quality 20-inch bicycle—like that on a good-quality adult bike—is not on a pivot (as it is on low-quality bikes), but is mounted on two horizontal rails so it can be moved forward and backward by an inch or so when the appropriate bolt is loosened. The test for proper position is the same as that used for adults. Tie a weighted string around the child's upper calf just below the knee, then have the child move that leg's pedal so it is in the forward horizontal position. The string should fall from the knee directly over the ball of the foot (see fig. 1-4). If it does not, the saddle position should be adjusted.

A child large enough to fit a 24-inch bicycle or an adult-sized bicycle should be fitted for a bike the same way as an adult (see Chapter 1). Just make sure the seat post is long enough to accommodate future growth—and every time the saddle must be raised, also check its horizontal placement.

## Eliminating Saddle Soreness

Be sensitive to any complaints from a child of any age about discomfort or aching in the saddle region. As any adult cyclist can attest, saddle soreness can be quite painful, and it does not always reveal itself in visible inflammation.

If the child complains of soreness primarily in one spot near the front of the crotch over the pubic bone, try tilting the saddle's nose downward a smidge to relieve pressure. If the soreness is primarily in two spots, one on either side of the crotch between the legs and toward the rear, it may be due to slight bruising of the tissues over the ischial tuberosities (sit bones). Visit a bike shop to see about getting a gel-filled pad for cushioning the saddle, or even a proper pair of padded cycling shorts (see "Necessary Accessories for 'Stokids'" in Chapter 3). Unless the child has toughed out the discomfort for so long that there is temporary tissue injury, relief should be nearly instantaneous.

## BUY QUALITY FOR SAFETY AND DURABILITY

Buying quality has already been emphasized for parents' bicycles and for trailers and child seats. If possible, it's even more vital for children's bicycles. Older kids are naturally hard on bikes: throwing them down onto the sidewalk, riding off curbs and down concrete stairs, popping wheelies and laying scratch and—well, just being kids.

You want to purchase equipment that can stand up to that kind of abuse—brake levers made of metal instead of plastic, chains that don't stretch and fall off, gear teeth that don't break off, headsets that don't lose a grip on the handlebars, spokes that don't pull through the wheel rims, wheel rims that don't crack.

If you have two or three kids spaced several years apart, you also want the bikes outgrown by the oldest child to be able to withstand the same abuse from all the younger siblings in succession—the same hand-me-down principle as with clothes. Even if you have only one child, buying durable bikes will enable you to recoup some fraction of your investment by selling each outgrown size to a neighbor with a smaller child.

For that kind of rugged durability, you must buy quality. "Toy stores and department stores want you to buy a new bicycle for your child's sixth birthday . . . and for the seventh birthday, and for the eighth birthday, and for the ninth birthday," noted Rick Politz, owner of bicycle shops in the Pennsylvania towns of Harleysville and Trappe. "So their bicycles are made to last about a year. A good-quality bicycle, though, should last through *all* the kids in a family."

Even for a child as young as three, go to a real bike shop, where a bicycle is not treated as a toy. The issue here is basic safety. Some 12-inch and 16-inch bicycles at toy stores are not even marketed as bicycles, but as "two-wheeled toys," in part to exempt them from stringent federal regulations on minimum requirements for bicycles—including the necessity for brakes and reflectors.

Quality is essential for one other reason: some cheap low-quality bicycles have a frame geometry and headset design that does not even allow a child to balance!

## HOW TO BUY QUALITY SECONDHAND

Let's face it, new bicycles are expensive. If even a bicycle shop's autumn discount prices are beyond affordability, however, consider buying used equipment. You can get high-quality bicycles for about a third the price of new if you're an astute judge of secondhand equipment.

Shopping for a secondhand bicycle is not at all like shopping for a new one. Forget being choosy about color or styling—all that counts is basic quality, mechanical condition, and acceptable fit.

Young children outgrow 12- and 16-inch bicycles so fast—and ride them so tentatively—that you are quite likely to find an outgrown smaller bike in good condition if it has been stored indoors. Finding a gently used 20-inch bike may be more of a challenge, as the original seven- to ten-year-old owner may have ridden it hard and maintained it poorly. But a previously owned 24-inch or adult-sized bike may be fine, as an older child or young teen may have cared for it responsibly.

Just as with buying a used car, the rule is "buyer beware": secondhand bikes are sold "as is" with no warranty and essentially no recourse in a return to the original owner. On the other hand, compared to cars, bicycles are mechanically simple and relatively easy and cheap to fix.

### Where to Look

The least risky place to look for a good-quality used child's bicycle is on the sales floor of an especially large bicycle shop that accepts trade-ins or offers to sell used bikes on consignment for members of an attached club. Look also in the classified section of the newsletter of a local bicycle club or a regional bicycling or multisport newspaper distributed to bicycle shops. Some local bike clubs may host a yearly swap meet. And in some regions of the nation famed as sport meccas, you may find entire stores that specialize in selling used or reconditioned athletic equipment.

Used kids' bikes from such sources are likely to have been owned by families of experienced cyclists who cared about the equipment, and are thus probably in as good condition as a secondhand bicycle can be. The flip side is, the owners know their worth, and so they are likely to be as expensive as the market will bear—although still cheap compared to new.

Riskier sources of secondhand kids' bikes are classified ads in your town's local newspaper, or at yard, garage, or tag sales. A little-known fact is that you can also buy bicycles at police auctions—periodic fund-raising auctions of unclaimed found or confiscated property, where the owners could not be traced. Yard-sale and police-auction bikes run the gamut in quality and condition, ranging from top models in mint condition to discount outlet specials that have been left out in the rain. So you really need to be an astute judge of quality and condition.

If you're vigilant, you may even find a used kid's bike for free on the street on regular garbage disposal days or on periodic "junk" or scavenger pickup days—scheduled disposal days in some communities for appliances, furniture, and other items that cannot be put into the normal trash. Scavenger days are usually publicized in advance; call your municipal government or local trash-disposal authority for details.

Many bicycles left out for junk day are in tough shape, otherwise their owners wouldn't have considered them to be garbage. But if you make a point of cruising around affluent neighborhoods where some people seem to think nothing of throwing out a perfectly good object just because they no longer want it, you may find a bike whose only problems are deteriorated tires and a dry, sagging chain.

### How to Evaluate Quality and Condition

One quick way of ascertaining the basic quality of a used kid's bike is by its decals. Look for bike-shop brands such as Giant, Mongoose, Raleigh, or Schwinn—and avoid department-store and toy-store brands (walk through bike shops and stores to make a list of yeas and nays).

If the bicycle's quality is good, then examine it carefully for mechanical condition. There are two show-stoppers for safety reasons: significant rust and a dented or bent frame.

Rust weakens metal. If the frame's paint is nearly absent, and the handlebar, chainwheels, and wheel rims are pitted with brown dots, forget it—the bicycle has been stored in a damp place or left outdoors in the rain. Worse than the visible rust may be unseen rust inside the hubs, headset, and bottom bracket—in fact, interior rust may even have eaten away the frame's tubing. It's unsafe for your child.

If the bike is not rusted, then sight along the tubes and carefully examine the paint: does the metal frame show any signs of having been dented, bent, or bent and then straightened? If so, then the metal has been irremediably weakened. Forget it. It's unsafe for your child.

If the bicycle is both of good quality and in safe mechanical shape, then check to make sure the expensive parts of the bike (front fork, headset, bottom bracket, derailleurs, wheels, hubs, saddle) are in acceptable condition. Basically, you want to wiggle all bearings and attachment points to make sure all parts are seated firmly.

To check the front fork and headset (where the handlebars are inserted into the steerer tube), grip the front wheel between your calves or knees and try to twist and lift up on the handlebars. To check the bottom bracket (where the pedals are inserted into the frame), take hold of the pedal cranks and try to move them left and right away from the frame, perpendicular to their plane of rotation. In both examinations, you should feel no sloppy looseness, grinding sensations, or slight clicking movements.

Next, carefully examine the chainwheel(s) and rear cog or freewheel cogs for broken or worn teeth, which would be moderately expensive to replace. For a derailleur bicycle, check to make sure that derailleurs are securely attached to the frame and that the bicycle can be shifted through all its gears.

Then check the wheels: make sure there are no broken spokes, that the wheels appear to be perfectly circular and rotate in one flat plane (that is, are both radially and laterally true). If the bicycle has hand brakes, make sure that a wheel does not rub against one of the brakes during part of each rotation (a tip-off that the wheel may be out of true). Wiggle the wheels left and right to see that there is no suspicious looseness in the hubs where the wheels attach to the frame and fork.

If you do detect problems in any of these areas, they may or may not indicate the necessity of major repairs. If you like the bike otherwise, see if you can make your final sale contingent on a full examination by a bike-shop mechanic.

If the bike passes all the important mechanical tests, don't be deterred by highly visible cosmetic flaws such as cracked or brittle tires, hardened brake pads, loose gear or brake cables, or a dry and squeaky chain. Those parts all normally age or wear, and are easy and cheap to replace. Missing or broken front, rear, and spoke reflectors are also inexpensive to replace. If it's evident that you'll have to spend money to replace worn items, you may be able to haggle down the price a few dollars.

Similarly, don't be stopped if the brake hoods (where the brake levers attach to the handlebar) are loose, or if the chain of a derailleur bicycle keeps jumping off the chainwheel sprockets or freewheel cogs when the bike is shifted into the highest or lowest gears. Chances are, the problem can be fixed by a quarter-turn of an appropriate screw.

## CARE AND FEEDING

Now that your child has a nice bicycle in great shape, encourage the same kind of pride and responsibility in caring for it as is customarily required for a new pet.

A well-maintained bicycle is a safe bicycle. A child with a bicycle whose handlebar twists in the headset, whose saddle keeps tipping up or back, whose seat post keeps sliding down into the seat tube, and whose chain is so loose and rusted it keeps falling off, is a child who is always on the brink of a serious accident. Part of the child's attention will always be distracted from the road and its traffic to the trickery of simply getting his/her machinery to function. Worse, a wreck of a bicycle may not allow the child to avoid danger at the next unexpected appearance of a dog or car, because the front wheel may not steer, the coaster brake may not grab, or the child's balance may be thrown off by the shifting saddle. Don't let poor maintenance put your child at risk.

A well-maintained bicycle is also a fun bicycle. It's no fun to ride a clunker that squeaks all the time, that is so rusted that every turn of the pedals is hard work, whose chain keeps falling off or skipping gears, whose brakes don't stop when you want them to, and whose handlebars and seat keep shifting out of position. A poorly maintained bicycle is nothing but frustrating and slow, and can even lead a child to think, "I'm not good enough to keep up with my friends." A well-maintained bicycle, on the other hand, is a joy to ride—smooth, silent, fast, responsive, cornering with a thrill, racing like the wind, eating up distance effortlessly, hopping curbs at will, taking on almost its own lithe animal spirit. This is what bicycling should be!

Perhaps most important, learning proper maintenance teaches a child independence and responsibility. As a child becomes familiar with the bike's parts and how they sound and feel (especially when they are in top condition), he or she will gradually come to sense when everything is working right and when it is not. In an emergency, this knowledge may give the child sufficient savvy to figure out enough of a roadside repair to get home. At the least, the child will come to know when the bike should be examined by a shop mechanic. By the time a child is a teen, he or she may have become a knowledgeable consumer for buying the final size of bicycle—the expensive one that may last through high school, college, and beyond.

The best form of maintenance is preventive. Teach your children to prevent or fix small problems before they become big, expensive problems.

**1.** Be firm about making each child—even the youngest—responsible for parking his or her bicycle indoors in a dry place every evening. Consistently insist that it be put there each evening before dinner is served.

Persistent dampness is the biggest enemy of a bicycle's metal and rubber parts, as well as of any accessories. Leaving a bicycle outdoors exposed to dew or rain can turn a $200-to-$500 investment into rusted, seized, mildewed, cracked, unridable junk in one season (see fig. 4-6). Even if it's not raining, dew can condense on the frame and chain, resulting in rust, which will eventually ruin every moving part. Such corrosion is even faster in the salty air near an ocean.

Most open or screened-in porches are not dry enough; yours is only if rain does not blow in, condensation does not form on the furniture, and there is no musty smell. Even covering the bike with a plastic sheet is no solution, as the sheet itself can trap condensation underneath. A detached garage or an unfinished basement is acceptable, if you know it's not damp or you keep a dehumidifier running twenty-four hours a day.

The best places to keep a bike are an attached garage, an enclosed summer porch, a finished basement (especially one waterproofed using a French drain system), or a spare room inside the house. Choose a storage place where the bicycles are easily accessible. If you always have to climb up a ladder to get one down from a rack above a doorway or from the garage rafters, you and your children simply won't use them—or will become careless about storage again.

*Figure 4-6. These snow-covered children's bicycles are being destroyed by neglect. For maximum life, bicycles should be stored indoors.*

*Figure 4-7. Recommended air pressure is indicated on the sidewall of each bicycle tire.*

2. Get older children into the routine of giving their bikes a Friday-after-school maintenance check before the weekend's fun. Encourage your child to become aware of the bicycle's normal feel and sounds—preferably after the bicycle has been over-hauled at a shop so the child gets used to it at its best. As soon as the child thinks something "feels funny" (extra rubbing or other resistance, unfamiliar clicks or squeaks, slipping or slightly wiggling parts), he or she should show you right away.

   To help children learn to diagnose problems, go over the bicycle together as if you were inspecting a secondhand bike you're thinking of buying (see "How to Evaluate Quality and Condition" above). There are also many excellent books describing routine bicycle maintenance, even for self-described ten-fingered klutzes (see Appendix 3).

   At the weekly maintenance check, have children pump up their tires to the rated pressure. Point out that the suggested tire pressure or range of pressures is printed on a label affixed to or embossed in the sidewall of each tire (see fig. 4-7). Show each child how to check the air pressure with a floor pump that has a built-in air-pressure gauge (a floor pump is a pump set on the floor and anchored with one foot while a handle is repeatedly raised and pushed down vertically to force air into a tire). If mountain-bike or BMX tires specify a range (say, "45 to 65 psi"), pump the tires up to the higher pressure for riding on pavement (the lower pressure is for greater traction for off-road riding).

A weekly tire-pressure check is essential because rubber inner tubes are slightly porous. After just one week of sitting, tubes will lose about a third of their pressure. After two or three weeks, even a child can feel that the tires are soft. After a season, the tires are totally flat.

Properly inflated tires require the least effort to pedal and so are the most fun to ride (when tires are squishy, the rider's weight compresses them so that more of their surface contacts the road, increasing rolling resistance). Properly inflated tires resist flats (under the pressure of riding, a too-soft inner tube can be pinched between rim and tire, resulting in a type of puncture known as a pinch flat). Properly inflated tires are a bicycle's only shock absorbers (a too-soft tire will allow the impact of a curb or pothole to dent the wheel's metal rim—possibly lessening braking effectiveness as well as the hold of the rim on the tire itself, creating the potential for a blowout).

*Note:* Caution your child not to exceed the recommended pressure when inflating a tire. The friction created by riding and braking—particularly on a hot day—heats the air inside the tires, increasing its pressure. If over-inflated, the inner tube can literally explode—which could be dangerous on a long downhill run. For the same reason, inflating bicycle tires with the air compressor at a gas station is not recommended. The air rushes out far too fast and the compressor's pressure gauge is not calibrated high enough for use on bicycle tires. If you have no other choice, inflate the bicycle tire only in tiny, tiny bursts.

3. Teach your kids to clean and lubricate their bicycles. Show your child how to brush the worst of the dirt from the chain after each ride—especially if you live in an area with sandy soil or if your children like to ride on dirt roads, on trails, or on the beach. Keep a soft cotton rag handy just for the purpose—an old T-shirt or part of an old cotton flannel nightgown is perfect. (Do not use paper towels—they shred instead of cleaning.)

Dirt is as abrasive as sandpaper. If dirt is allowed to build up on a bicycle chain, braking (for a coaster-brake bicycle) or shifting (for a derailleur bicycle) becomes sloppy, unreliable, and really annoying. On a derailleur bicycle, grit on the chain grinds away at the gear sprockets, slowly but surely wearing down the metal teeth of these expensive parts. (Given proper care, chain-wheel and freewheel gears should last 10,000 to 15,000 miles.)

If the chain starts to squeak, show your child how to put the tiniest drop of motor oil, tenacious oil (sold in bike shops), or other light machine oil into each link (do not use vegetable-based 3-in-1 oil, which will gunk up the works). Then—and this step is important—take a clean cotton rag and wipe off any excess oil from the outside of the chain, to avoid attracting any more dirt than necessary.

Chains stretch with use, having a limited life of perhaps only 1,000 to 2,000 miles. A stretched chain no longer meshes prop-erly with the gear teeth, giving rise to sloppy shifting and grinding down of the gear teeth. There are tests to see if a chain has stretched and needs to be replaced, but why bother? Chains are cheap. Keep life simple: each spring, replace the chain of every bicycle. In fact, each spring have a local shop give every bicycle a thorough safety check and tune-up.

The best grease-cutter for children to use to clean the frame and the wheel rims of a bicycle is good old rubbing alcohol. It is cheap, readily available at pharmacies and grocery stores, and nontoxic (if not imbibed)—and it evaporates cleanly, leaving no residue. Make sure, however, that the kids work with adequate ventilation, as alcohol is flammable.

The best grease-cutters for getting chain grease off skin—better even than products advertised just for that purpose—are baby diaper wipes that contain lanolin. Keep a full-sized container on your workbench and carry the travel size on your rides.

4. Take an introductory bicycle maintenance course with your child(ren). You and your child(ren) don't need to know every-thing about fixing bicycles—just enough not to be stranded by a common mishap. Good, simple introductions are offered all over the country by local bike clubs and shops, YMCAs, chapters of the American Youth Hostels, and adult education centers. In about five class hours plus practice, you and any child of ten or twelve should be able to learn how to repair a flat tire, adjust a rubbing brake, adjust the front or rear derailleur, jury-rig a broken spoke until you can reach a shop, and rejoin a broken chain.

In addition to the knowledge you'll gain from taking such a

course, you'll also gain peace of mind. You'll feel more confident about taking your family on longer bicycle trips—or letting your older kids go off riding on their own—if you know that everyone can get rolling again after a minor breakdown.

## HELMETS FOR SCHOOL-AGED CHILDREN

A helmet can make the difference between a fall resulting in a concussion or worse—or in just some pulled neck muscles and a scary story. Most fatalities on bicycles are from head injuries—and eighty-five percent of those could have been prevented if the cyclist had been wearing a helmet. Consider this chilling fact: a child doesn't even need to be riding the bicycle in order to fall hard enough to incur permanent brain damage. If a child falls over from standing height even while stopped astride the bicycle, a direct blow to the temple could kill. Vertical height counts for as much as forward velocity (see Chapter 2 for a full discussion of helmet safety standards).

The protection a helmet provides isn't expensive. A good helmet costs about the same as a good pair of children's shoes. And unlike shoes, each size of helmet should fit your child for several years (teenagers will probably wear a small adult size).

Since kids respond more strongly to the appearance of things than to their function, let your youngsters choose one they find "cool." Helmets for elementary-school-aged children are decorated in all their favorite designs, in neon colors, with imaginative characters. There are also helmets designed to accommodate pony tails. Let the helmet be a fashion accessory as well as a safety accessory. If a child likes the helmet, he or she will be eager to wear it—but if he or she doesn't like it, you may face a battle before every ride.

However "cool" the Darth Vader look may be, encourage your children to avoid black, which absorbs the sun's rays and can become very hot. Suggest that they consider white or yellow, which will make them more visible. For older kids who like daylong or weekend bicycle touring, note that some helmets can be fitted with optional plastic visors to keep sun and rain out of the eyes and off the nose.

*Caution:* Do not allow a child to substitute a helmet designed for football, baseball, or some other sport. Non-bicycling headgear may not be designed to protect the head at the speed or type of impact encountered while riding a bicycle.

Do not allow a child to use crayons, paints, or markers on a helmet, or to affix stickers to it; some solvents, dyes, or glues may cause a chemical interaction that may weaken the plastic of the outer shell.

Such alterations may also void the manufacturer's warranty.

Treat helmets with care! Do not allow children to play catch with helmets, or allow a helmet to fall from a height onto pavement. Repeated impacts may cause microscopic cracks that will give way right when the helmet's protection is needed most.

If your child should ever fall and the helmet does its job in protecting the head, retire the honorable helmet from service—especially if you see any scrape, ding, dent, or split in the outer shell or inner crushable foam. Some helmet manufacturers will award you a brand new helmet if you send them the damaged one with a complete description of the accident to aid in their continuing head-protection research. Read the literature inside the box or call the company for specific information.

## FITTING THE HELMET

The single most common error seen in child cyclists is that their helmets are far too loose and set too far back on the head (see fig. 4-8). The second most common error is that the chin strap is left unclipped. A helmet that is too loose or unclipped will *not* offer protection. Both helmet and strap must be tight to keep the helmet on the head should it hit more than once—say, a car first and then the road.

Check the snugness of the helmet with the same bend-over test recommended in Chapter 2 for toddlers. Have your child place the helmet on the head but leave the chin strap unfastened; then ask the child to bend forward and touch forehead to knees. The unfastened helmet should not fall off. If the helmet falls off, insert thicker fitting-sponges. If the helmet stays on, the fit is snug enough to be safe.

An alternative to the bend-over test is the fast-shake test. Set the helmet on the child's head with the chin strap unfastened. Then ask the child to shake his or her head from side to side vigorously, as if indicating an emphatic "No!" The helmet should stay firmly in place on the head. If it slides around, it's too loose.

Like an adult's helmet, helmets for school-aged children should cover the skull. The helmet's chin and side straps should be adjusted so the helmet stays level, just one or two finger-widths above the eyebrows (a locking feature inside some helmets helps keep it from rocking). When the straps are properly adjusted, the child should *not* be able to push the helmet back off the forehead. And, if the child walks toward a wall the helmet should touch before the child's nose.

On most good helmets, the chin straps attach to each side of the helmet in two places, so that each strap forms the letter "Y" when it hangs loose. A fastener at the center of each "Y" allows the length of the

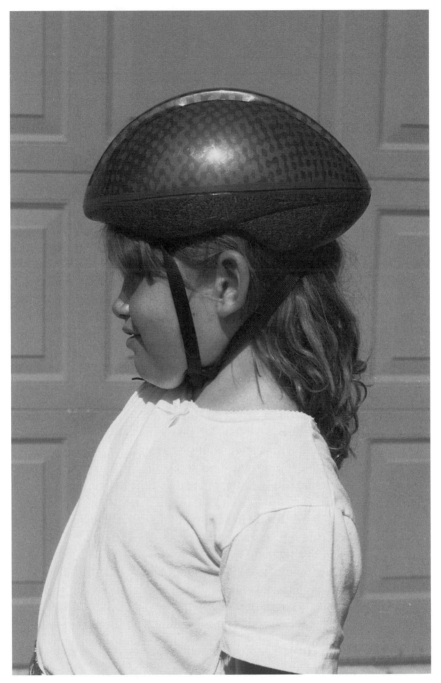

*Figure 4-8. The chin straps should be adjusted so the helmet sits level on the child's head (left); it should not be tilted back off the forehead (right).*

each of the two upper legs of the "Y" to be adjusted independently. The side straps should be adjusted so this fastener falls just under the earlobe.

The chin strap should be tightened until there is just enough room for one finger to be slipped between strap and jaw. The straps should return to their original position—firmly against the skin—when the finger is removed.

*Fig 4-9. Bind the hair of a long-haired child before riding to prevent crying later when painful knots must be combed out.*

As children grow you should expect to buy them two or three helmets. Whenever you buy a new helmet, save all the sizing sponges that come with it, especially if your child starts out needing the fattest set of sponges. Check the sizing sponges for proper fit at least twice a year, or when the child begins to complain that the helmet is too tight. As the child's head grows, substitute the successively thinner sponges for future adjustments. The child needs the next size larger helmet when even the thinnest fitting-sponges are too tight.

What to do with an outgrown helmet? Clean it with mild liquid dish detergent and warm water and save it for the next offspring—or for a young helmetless visitor whom you might want to have join you on a ride. Helmets are such personal items that used ones have no resale value through bike shops or club newsletters. Nor should you buy a used helmet at a yard sale: you never know whether it has been in a crash, and there have been rare cases of head lice transferred from one child to another through the trading of bicycle helmets.

The most important thing, of course, is that the child actually put on and fasten the helmet *every* time he or she mounts the saddle, no matter how short the ride, even if it's just on the sidewalk. A helmet is not talismanic—it does its owner's head no good if it is packed in a bookbag, dangling from a handlebar, or left home.

# Chapter 5

# Learning to Ride: Ready, Set, Balance!

Forget altogether the ways you were probably taught to ride a two-wheeler. The time-honored method is that Dad holds onto the saddle and runs alongside to propel the bike while exhorting the child to steer. The child doesn't control the bike—Dad does, and the moment Dad lets go is terrifying. This traditional cold-turkey method practically guarantees that a child will fall, with some nasty road rash if the fall is on pavement.

You should also forget another widely advocated alternative method: taking the child and the two-wheeler to the top of a grassy rise, pointing the youngster downhill, and promising prizes of gradually increasing value as he or she reaches successively farther distances (an M&M, a Lego, a nickel, an

Oreo cookie). While it does work after a while (as does Dad's traditional method), the child may not get the knack of balancing until after executing spinning falls at the ends of several dozen runs—crying furiously each time. Or after one or two spills the child may adamantly refuse to try again, and no prize may be a valuable enough bribe.

Last, forget the use of training wheels. Even a child who becomes a skilled and confident rider using training wheels may not have learned to balance—in fact, chances are, he or she has simply learned to ride while leaning on one training wheel as if it were the third wheel of a tricycle.

## BUILD CONFIDENCE FIRST

Both the "Dad" and the "downhill" methods are terrifying for kids not only because there is such a high risk of falling, but because both the ingredients they need to succeed are missing.

To ride a bicycle, every child needs to have both *control* and a *sense of control*. The first is the actual ability to do the job, and the second is the confidence to try. The two are mutually reinforcing. Succeeding a little gives the child a sense of mastery and pride, which encourages further attempts; more attempts means more practice, and practice makes perfect, engendering more confidence, and so it goes. Learning becomes efficient and positive.

Of these two requirements, confidence must come first. If a child is so fearful that he or she refuses even to try, then there is no possibility of tasting success and beginning to learn actual control. On the other hand, if a child really wants to learn—and fundamentally believes that he or she can learn—then, despite even severe handicaps, that child will persist and eventually will learn.

An important part of encouraging confidence involves directly addressing fears rather than passing them off. If your child keeps crying, "I'm scared! I'm scared!" then listen and find out why. Chances are, the child's biggest fear is of falling—of getting hurt.

The child's fear of getting hurt can be allayed by a combination of protective equipment and positive propaganda. When my daughter, Roxana, was five, she would not consent to riding even with training wheels until I had fitted her out with the elbow and knee pads used by in-line skaters—in addition to the helmet and padded cycling gloves she already owned. As soon as she put them on, I praised her for how "cool" and "athletic" she looked. I also told her the pads would keep her from getting hurt should she fall—that they were like helmets for her elbows and knees. This little pep talk gave her at least enough confidence to give this bicycle-riding business a shot. Other cycling parents have chosen to teach their children to ride in late winter or very early spring, when the weather is still cold enough for the child to be bundled up in a padded snowsuit.

But the best way to address a child's fear of falling is by teaching a child to ride in a way that minimizes the chance of falling.

## WHY TRAINING WHEELS *DON'T* WORK

For decades, parents have been led to believe that using training wheels—two small wheels mounted on brackets, one on each side of the axle of the bicycle's rear wheel—will allow a child to learn to ride naturally. The training wheels hold the bicycle upright so that a child can ride the bicycle right away without learning to balance. As the weeks go by, the training wheels are gradually raised, so that, theoretically, the child is compelled to balance in order to keep the bicycle upright—but in the event of losing his or her balance will be caught and saved from falling by the little wheels. At some magical point, the parent can remove one or both training wheels, and *Voilà!* Off the child rides into the sunset, perfectly balanced. In practice, the theory seldom works (which is why many parents resort to Dad's terrifying technique).

Training wheels present several problems. First, unless you live in a new housing development where the newly laid sidewalks are absolutely flat, training wheels keep catching on every irregularity and suspending the chain-driven rear wheel in mid-air—a constant interruption that will simply frustrate the child (see fig. 5-1). On any

*Figure 5-1. Training wheels can hang up in minor cracks or rough spots, causing the child to lift or drag the bicycle.*

bike that will be ridden on the uneven sidewalks common in older sub-urbs, the training wheels must be raised at least half an inch right from the start so the bicycle already feels "tippy" and insecure.

Second, each time the training wheels are raised, the bicycle will feel even more "tippy," making some children feel insecure all over again and thus reluctant to ride. In an attempt to regain stability, the child may lean the bicycle so it rides on just one of the training wheels—thereby turning the bike into a tricycle. Even with the training wheels raised to their highest position, some children become adept at riding while canted 15 degrees off vertical and thus have still not learned to balance the bicycle (see fig. 5-2).

Finally, raised training wheels may cause accidents rather than preventing them. A turning bicycle naturally banks into the turn. In an intentionally sharp turn, a raised training wheel may catch on the ground, surprising the child and perhaps causing a spill. Making a sharp turn on a bike with training wheels requires that a child lean away from the turn rather than into it—which instills incorrect expectations for riding a two-wheeler.

For these and other reasons, many cycling parents view train-ing wheels as a crutch that actually *retards* a child's learning to ride a bike. In their view, the only way a child can learn to balance a two-wheeler is by learning on two wheels instead of four.

That being said, training wheels can play a helpful role in three very limited ways. First, by affording stability, they can encourage a cau-tious or timid child to try riding at all. Second, they allow this same child to feel stable enough to ride at a speed fast enough that balancing on two wheels is even possible (dispense with training wheels as soon as the child is comfortable at riding at a good clip, around 6 miles per hour, or the speed of a jogging adult). Third, training wheels make it easier to learn how to use the brakes—a skill that must become reflex before the child learns to balance (see below).

If your child is not timid by nature, however, don't bother with training wheels at all: go directly to the real thing—a gentle method whereby the child can learn to balance and ride without falling.

## PREPARING TO LEARN

First, find a good place to practice. Look for a section of smooth pavement a block or two long in a place free of traffic, dogs, joggers, or other distractions, where the child does not have to pay attention to the direction he or she is headed. Ideal choices include a dead-end street, a blacktopped school playground, or a parking lot abandoned on the

weekend. Most residential driveways are too short and narrow; even on a one hundred-foot-long drive, the child will have just reached a good speed when he or she will be forced to stop or turn, and thus will never get the chance to practice essential skills for a protracted distance.

Next, make sure that both you and your child are properly fitted with helmets—and wear them right from the very first practice. Have even the most adventurous child wear a long-sleeved sweatshirt and long pants to minimize scrapes in a fall.

## THE "BBP NO-FALL METHOD"

The most thoughtful and considered method for teaching children to ride is the sequence of steps developed by John P. Waterman, director of The Arc Cycling Program in Westland, Michigan. Since 1988, he has used his method with great success to teach bicycling to hundreds of adults and children with disabilities ranging from autism to Down syndrome to cerebral palsy. Waterman's method squares well with independent suggestions offered by other parents, bike-shop owners and mechanics, other cycling experts, physical education specialists, and my own observations and experimentation.

Waterman breaks the tasks of bicycling down into specific skills, which should be taught in the order of "brakes, balance, and pedal." One can remember the initials "BBP" as a handy mnemonic. Because this sequence minimizes the child's chances of falling, a good name seems to be the "BBP No-Fall Method."

### Brakes: First Learn to Stop

First teach the child how to stop the bicycle using the brakes.

Why start with stopping?

Many accidents with children happen because a kid simply freezes into inaction. And if he or she is coasting down a driveway into the street or down a grassy slope toward a tree, that can spell disaster. Even a toy bicycle with tiny 12-inch wheels can roll faster than many adults can run. Therefore, before a child is taught how to propel the bike forward, it is important that he or she develop both the knowledge and the reflexes to stop at will.

For best results, don't teach a child to stop by using the coaster brakes that are standard on most kids' bikes. Instead, have a bike shop

Figure 5-2. Even with training wheels raised to the highest position, some children resist learning to balance and lean on one wheel, becoming adept at riding canted 15 degrees off vertical.

install small hand brakes. To set good habits from the start, make sure the shop installs the brakes in the configuration standard with all adult bicycles: the right lever operating the rear brake and the left lever operating the front brake.

Why are hand brakes superior to coaster brakes?

Using foot brakes, as Waterman points out, requires that a child must stop doing one thing (pedaling forward) in order to do something else quite different (pedal backward). This complex switch is harder for a child to master than simply doing another task—in this case, squeezing the fingers, which has the added benefit of being a natural fright reflex.

Second, foot-operated coaster brakes do not have a freewheel. Thus, a child cannot backpedal to put a pedal in the right position for mounting or dismounting the bicycle.

Third, hand brakes are intrinsically safer. Hand brakes are faster to activate: all it takes is a quick finger grab as opposed to making the legs do a 180-degree backpedal. Hand-brake pads grip better than the internal mechanism in the coaster-brake hub, stopping the bike faster in dry conditions. The child can stop while still seated, maintaining a stable low center of gravity, while a fast stop with coaster brakes may require the child to stand up to really stomp on the pedals. Gripping the hand brakes holds the bike still while dismounting; coaster brakes are disengaged the instant the child steps off one pedal at a stop, allowing the bicycle to start to roll—possibly causing a pedal to scrape the back of the standing ankle. Worse, if the chain should fall off a coaster-brake bike—a common occurrence on cheap toy-store or department-store bikes—the child has no brake at all; hand brakes are unaffected by the chain. Last, hand brakes help even small children develop the hand strength and skill needed to operate the hand brakes they'll find on bigger bikes.

Hand brakes can be mastered while the child is using training wheels. Use the smooth blacktop of a playground, and encourage the child to start and stop. Make a game of it. Lay sticks or draw chalk lines at which the child has to stop. After that level is mastered, let the child get up a real head of steam, and then shout "Stop!" Measure reaction time by how far the child travels before coming to a halt.

Next, take your own bicycle and ride around the blacktop with the child, pretending that tetherball poles or other playground structures are stop signs. An advanced game is for you to roll a ball in front of the child unexpectedly, to see how reflexively the child stops.

When you are satisfied that the child has good instinctive mastery of the brakes, remove the training wheels and move on to the second step.

## *Balance: Ride on Two Wheels Without Falling*

Learning to balance on two wheels is hard because a bicycle is intrinsically more stable at higher speeds (above 6 or 7 mph) than it is at lower speeds (2 or 3 mph). The problem is, to most beginners faster speeds feel scarier, and they prefer to ride slowly. But riding slowly is exactly when the bike is the most unstable and feels "tippy." In fact, the bike's instability at low speeds is why mounting (getting on before it falls over) and dismounting (getting off before it falls over) are also challenging to master.

So how can a child learn to balance a bike at slow speeds without falling?

First, the child needs to develop the feel of balancing when the bicycle is stationary. To do this, temporarily turn the bike into a scooter. Remove both pedals and lower the height of the bike's saddle so that the child can easily straddle it: Waterman recommends that the feet should rest flat on the ground when the child is sitting on the saddle. (*Note:* This unnaturally low position should be assumed *only* for the duration of the learning, *not* for actual riding.) Alternatively, have the child learn to ride on a bicycle that is a size too small. Before proceeding, also lower the seat on your own bike.

Ask the child to hold the bicycle stationary by squeezing the hand brakes (note that the removal of the pedals will have disabled any coaster brake), and to sit on the saddle with feet lightly touching the ground. Then ask the child to raise the feet an inch while trying to keep the bicycle balanced vertically.

Seated on your own bike, show the child the essential trick for balancing: if the bicycle begins to fall, twitch the front wheel to steer *in the direction of the fall* (see fig. 5-3). If the bike starts falling to the right, turn the front wheel to the right; if the bike starts falling to the left, turn to the left. If all else fails, put your feet down—but not before trying to correct the fall. Count aloud to make a game of seeing how long the child can keep the bicycle balanced at a standstill before needing to touch down an outstretched toe. Never touch the child's bike during any training session—the object of the lesson is to make the child feel in control.

Two exercises, devised by Reginald Joules of Denver, Colorado, further help a child learn the fundamentals of balancing when the bicycle is stationary. Joules's "pedal magic" approach (as he calls it) differs from Waterman's in that Joules leaves the pedals attached and the parent controls the bicycle.

For Joules's "tilt and turn" exercise, have the child sit astride the bicycle with the feet on the pedals while you stand behind, holding the

*Figure 5-3. When a bicycle tips off the vertical in one direction (A), teach a child to recover his or her balance by twitching the front wheel in the same direction (B).*

bicycle upright. Explain that as you lean the bicycle to the left, the child should turn the handlebars to the left; as you lean the bicycle to the right, the child should turn the handlebars to the right. Reassure the child that you have full control of the bicycle and will not let it fall, so the child should keep the feet on the pedals. Then announce the direction of each lean and see whether the child responds quickly and correctly.

Once it's clear the child has the hang of it—which may take only a few minutes—graduate to the "random rock" exercise, in which you do not announce the direction of the lean, but the child has to respond reflexively by turning the handlebars in the correct direction. Once the child has responded without error for twenty "random rocks" in a row, in Joules's experience the child has internalized the basics of balance and is ready to ride.

When the child has mastered balancing at a standstill, suggest that it would be fun to try balancing while moving. On a level section of the practice area, encourage the seated child to try propelling the bicycle forward by "walking" it with the outstretched feet. Remind the child that stopping requires just a squeeze of the hand-brake levers. If the child is hesitant, point out that he or she will not fall, as the out-stretched feet will touch the ground before the bicycle tips too far. (Joules's technique bypasses "walking the bike"; he has found that many children can go directly to pedaling the bike around a parking lot. Waterman's more gradual approach, however, is useful for children needing more confidence as well as for children having difficulty learning to balance.)

Demonstrate the movement yourself by shoving off with your feet, perhaps with a well-placed "Whee-e!" It won't take much encour-agement; as your child gets used to the posture and the movement, he or she will playfully start to give the bike harder pushes. Each stride of the "walking" will start to become longer and longer until it's almost like slow-motion running (see fig. 5-4). Challenge: "Can you do these big,

*Figure 5-4. Encourage the child to balance a moving bicycle by sitting on the lowered saddle and propelling the bike with "big, funny giant steps."*

funny giant steps?" The child will probably start laughing at the new feeling of speed, which is completely under the child's control. Just to keep the braking practice also in mind, occasionally shout "Stop!" Both of you should then stop by gripping the hand brakes. Encourage the child to shout "Stop!" unexpectedly to catch you out in turn.

When it is clear that the child is thoroughly comfortable with this game—a good clue is if he or she seems a little bit bored or expresses the wish that it were more exciting—add a new challenge. "Can you do this trick?" You should now "run" your bicycle until it is moving rapidly and then—keeping your legs close to the frame—bend your knees and lift your feet about 6 inches off the ground. Coast in that position a few moments before touching the ground again. Monkey-see, monkey-do, your child will try the same—and will likely succeed (remember, a bicycle is most stable at high speed). Once the child loses any sign of hesitancy or instability, start a contest to see who can keep their feet up the longest at high speed.

Last, graduate to a contest of who can keep their feet up the longest at *slow* speed, coasting great lengths to let the bicycles come nearly to a stop. Encourage the child to keep the knees tucked in, close to the bike frame, not stuck out wide. Balancing at low speed with the legs held in is harder and may take longer to master, but it is essential for learning enough control to mount and dismount. As a game, suggest a "slow race" to see who can take the longest to cover a certain distance.

At this point your child has mastered balancing on two wheels! Congratulations are in order!

### Pedal: Mount, Dismount, Pedal

Once the child can balance, it's time to teach him or her to mount and dismount the bicycle.

Teaching a child to mount and dismount correctly is essential if the child is to be able to ride with the saddle at the correct height for full leg extension (that is, with legs nearly straight at the bottom of the pedal stroke). Many kids, if left to their own devices, take to sitting on the saddle and shoving the bike forward with their feet, putting the feet on the pedals only when the bike is going fast enough to be balanced. When the saddle is low enough for the child to reach the ground, however, it is too low for proper leg extension: the leg is still bent at a 90-degree angle at the bottom of the pedal stroke, and is folded up toward the chest at the top (see fig. 5-5). This position is highly uncomfortable and tiring for riding any real distance.

Figure 5-5. If the saddle is low enough for the child to touch the ground while seated (top), the child will not have proper leg extension while riding (bottom).

*Figure 5-6. When the saddle is high enough to afford the child proper leg extension (top), it will be too high for the child to touch the ground while seated (bottom).*

A saddle height that is correct for proper leg extension will be too high for the child to touch the ground at all while seated (see fig. 5-6). To accustom the child to a position that more closely approximates proper saddle height, Waterman recommends installing just one pedal and starting to inch up the height of the saddle so that the ground is accessible only on tiptoe. After each raise of the saddle, the child might want to repeat some of the earlier exercises, such as the long funny giant steps, to be reassured that no knowledge has been forgotten even though the bike feels different.

Which pedal should you install first? The right one, if you live in the United States or anywhere where people drive on the right side of the road. Why? Roads are crowned—raised in the center and lower at the sides—to shed water. According to John Forester in his classic book *Effective Cycling,* in the United States, where bicycles legally ride on the right side of the road with traffic, you want to push off (mount) with your left foot on the ground, which will have a higher and more stable position; likewise, you want to step down (dismount) with your left foot. Let's literally get the child started off on the right foot.

Now, with the right pedal installed, encourage the child to begin mounting properly. Demonstrate yourself by rolling your bicycle forward—or backpedaling on the freewheel—until the right pedal is in the power position: just forward of the top of the stroke at about the two o'clock position. Stand over the frame of the bike; do not sit on the saddle (on a properly fitting bike, you won't be able to, anyway). Rest the right foot on the pedal. Then push down on the pedal with the right foot while, simultaneously, pushing your body up off the ground with your left, seating yourself on the saddle. After demonstrating a couple of times, coach your child to do the same (see fig. 5-7).

Also encourage the child to coast slowly to a stop to practice dismounting. As the bike slows to a halt, the child should stand up, putting all his or her weight on the pedal (right foot), squeeze the hand brakes, and step down to the ground with the left foot (see fig. 5-8).

Install the second (left) pedal only after the child has mastered mounting and dismounting. Repeat the same basic exercises (contests, games)—long funny giant steps, braking, mounting, dismounting—while keeping the feet on the pedals instead of just held off the ground. You can even begin to award points: the longer the feet are on the pedals, the more points are awarded.

The aim of this exercise is to develop self-confidence more than skill. While the level of control needed to keep the feet on the pedals is not any greater than that needed to hold the feet above the ground, the

Figure 5-7. Teach the child how to mount the bicycle properly. Start with the right pedal raised to the power position with the right foot resting on the pedal (1). In one motion, push down on the pedal with the right foot to propel the bicycle forward while pushing the body up off the ground with the left foot (2). Then sit on the saddle (3).

Figure 5-8. Teach the child how to dismount the bicycle properly. While squeezing the brake levers to stop the bicycle (1), slide forward off the saddle to stand on the right pedal, which will be at the bottom of the pedal stroke (2). When the bicycle is nearly stopped, keep squeezing the brake levers and step down to the ground with the left foot (3).

child's *sense* of control must be greater; a child still feeling uncertain of his or her control feels safer holding the feet just over the ground than placing them on the pedals.

As their confidence increases, children should be encouraged to begin pedaling. At this point the child may start zipping around faster than he or she can run. Continue to shout "Stop!" now and then to encourage practice in braking and dismounting at higher speeds.

## PUTTING IT ALL TOGETHER

Advanced practice in both balance and pedaling can be gained by learning to turn. On a bike, turning is done as much by leaning the body as by turning the handlebars. Start by asking the child to make big circles to the right and then to the left. As the child gains confidence, encourage him or her to make smaller circles (sharper turns). Coach the child to keep the pedal on the inside of the turn raised so it won't drag on the ground and cause a spill.

As soon as a child starts to show off, challenge him or her to execute all kinds of fancy S-turns, working up to doing vigorous right and left turns in quick succession. Make it extra fun by placing bright yellow tennis-ball halves, kitchen sponges, empty soft-drink cans, or other markers on the ground as a kind of slalom course through which the child steers. The idea is for the child to feel out the limits of the bicycle and to practice steering in the direction of incipient falls.

Once your son or daughter seems stable and confident on the level at all speeds with feet on the pedals, suggest coasting down a grassy hill. If the response is enthusiastically positive, then go partway up the gentle rise.

This next exercise is qualitatively different from all the previous ones and you need to prepare your child in advance. Say something like: "On level ground, we've had total control over how fast we want to go. But when you coast down this hill, gravity will be helping you. That makes this ride a little more exciting. If you want to slow down or stop, what do you do?" If you've done your job well, the child will pipe up: "Squeeze the brakes." "And when you want to get off at the end?" You'll know your child is ready if he or she can demonstrate a proper dismount.

Challenge the child to a pedaling race to the top of the rise (pedal makes perfect). Demonstrating with your own bike, coast down the slope with your feet on the pedals—a well-placed "Whee-ee!" might add to the fun. Then dismount at the bottom to watch your child's first solo ride down the slope (see fig. 5-9).

This is the first exercise in the BBP teaching method in which

*Figure 5-9. When the child feels he or she can balance on the flat, try heading down a gentle grassy slope at higher speed under the pull of gravity.*

the child has some risk of falling. The thrill of going downhill is so great, anything can happen. A child might well forget to steer or brake, or may take the feet off the pedals and try to stop by dragging them in the grass. While you should be prepared to catch the child if he or she completely loses balance when the bike slows down enough to stop, don't touch the child unless it's really necessary to prevent a fall: you want the child to be in control as much as possible. With any luck, the youngster will have integrated all the balancing, turning, braking, and correcting skills he or she has been practicing and will carry off the first downhill run with grace and aplomb. As confidence is gained, start farther and farther up the rise until the child is beginning from the crest.

Once all these goals have been met, reward your child with a bicycling-related graduation prize: a water bottle and cage, a basket, a horn.

## ADVANCED TRAINING: TEACHING A CHILD HOW TO SHIFT GEARS

Now that your child is ready to try some family bicycling adventures while riding independently, pass along a valuable tip: the key to lasting for a half-day or daylong bicycle trip is conserving energy.

If a child rides too fast early in the trip, he or she may well be dragging at the end. Teach children to pace themselves, riding slowly enough that conversation is easy without panting for breath.

Most novices on bicycles simply work too hard. Accustomed to pushing hard on the pedals—probably as a result of learning to ride on one-speed bicycles—they often ride in too high a gear. Now that it is possible to outfit even first-graders with real multigeared mountain bikes, instruction in how to take advantage of the marvelous leverage of a bicycle's lower gears to make pedaling as little work as possible can begin as early as age six or seven.

For most shifting, the child should use the right shift lever (the only one on a 20-inch mountain bike) to move the rear derailleur across the freewheel's cogs. One click of the shift lever corresponds to one change of gear. Remind the child that on a derailleur bicycle, the feet must be pedaling to shift gears.

How does the child know when he or she is riding in the right gear? For most terrain, the feet should be circling faster than once a second—even when going uphill. In cycling jargon, the child (and the parent) should maintain a high cadence—at least 60 to 90 rpm (revolutions per minute).

Yes, you and the child will feel as though you're hardly working: that's precisely the idea! When you pedal at high cadence, bicycling exercises the heart and lungs, and doesn't strain the knee joints and thigh muscles. High cadence takes advantage of the fact that the heart can recover from aerobic demands in a few minutes, while the thigh muscles (quadriceps) take forty-eight hours to recover from anaerobic strain. High cadence is the secret to enjoying a long ride, not dying on hills, and being eager and able to ride the bicycle the next day.

When a child graduates to a 12-speed bicycle with a double crank (two chainwheels or front sprockets), teach him or her to adjust the left shift lever to put the chain on the smaller of the two chainwheels for most riding. On a bicycle with 15 or more speeds, which has three chainwheels—a configuration known in bicycling jargon as a triple crank— (see fig. 5-10) have the child put the chain on the middle chainwheel. Then keep it there for most family riding over flat or gently rolling terrain (the large chainwheel will not be used except maybe on the fastest of downhills, when the child is a skilled rider).

Once you and your kids all have derailleur bicycles with triple cranks, you're set for nearly painless climbing of even considerable mountains. You just need to master a bit of timing for downshifting. When starting to head up a real climb, teach children to keep their cadence as

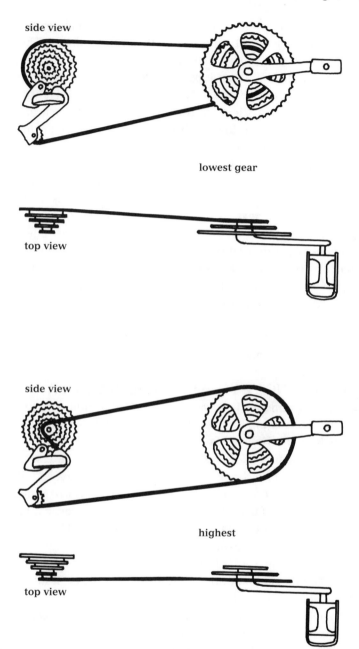

side view

lowest gear

top view

side view

highest

top view

*Figure 5-10. Lower (easier) gears are the ones closer to the bicycle frame—smaller chainwheel in front, larger cogs in the rear (top); higher (harder) gears are the ones farther from the bicycle frame—larger chainwheel in front, smaller cogs in the rear (bottom).*

high as possible: they should downshift into the next lower gear just as soon as they're exerting a bit more force than easy pedaling. They should *not* wait until they're pushing the pedals hard: at that point, so much force is put on the chain that it cannot be shifted to a lower gear—and they will have no choice but to get off and walk. Progressively downshift with the right-hand shift lever until you're in the lowest gear in the rear. Similarly, teach them to downshift (keep those pedals turning!) while approaching a stop sign or red light, so they do not try to start up again when in an impossibly high gear.

If even more leverage is necessary, adjust the left shift lever to drop the chain onto the smallest of the three chainwheels in front. Officially called an alpine gear, this powerful little cog is more widely known as a "granny gear." Your feet will spin and you will travel only as fast as you can walk. But you and your kids will ride up that hill with greater ease than any of you could push the bike on foot—essential for hauling any kind of load (full panniers or a child in a child seat or trailer).

You'll also get a wonderful aerobic workout. Pace yourself so you're breathing moderately—that is, you can still hold a conversation—and all of you will last until the crest. Once at the top, raise a water bottle in a toast to the view and your child's triumph.

## NON-BICYCLING TOYS: WINNER AND SINNER

Children as young as three can be proficient at riding on two wheels if given the right equipment—equipment that will encourage them to develop balance and sense of control.

One helpful non-bicycling toy is a scooter. The classic design hasn't changed in its essentials in over forty years. Between two wheels (one behind the other as on a bike) there is a narrow horizontal platform on which the child stands, while in front there is a vertical handle attached to the front wheel that allows the child to steer. High-end models even have pneumatic tires and hand brakes. While holding onto the handle, the child places one foot on the platform and uses the other to shove off the ground. Scooting along the sidewalk, even little kids can propel themselves faster than they can run.

Why a scooter? The sense of balance needed to keep a scooter upright is precisely the same as that needed to balance a bike. If anything, balancing a scooter may be slightly more demanding, as its movement left and right off the vertical is quicker than a bike's. A child can readily develop a feel for the balance point by standing with one foot on the platform and holding the other leg out slightly, ready to step down at the first quiver of instability. Many parents have found that children who cannot seem to manage balancing on a bicycle can do so readily after having mastered riding a scooter.

*Do not buy a tricycle.* Unlike a scooter—and contrary to popular belief—a trike is not a natural step to a bike. Tricycles handle differently from bicycles, as you will find if you have a go on an adult tricycle. From a bicyclist's viewpoint, the three-point stability that makes a trike easy to ride the first time is also its bane; as it requires no skill of its rider, it does nothing to develop a sense of balance. Moreover, the trike's pedals are attached to the axle of the front wheel, so every time a pedal is pushed, the steering is affected. The knees are bent in all positions of the pedal stroke so that there is no proper leg extension, setting a poor expectation for later bicycling. A trike has no brakes, so a child learns bad habits (such as dragging the feet to stop). Last, despite the trike's overt resemblance to a bike and its similar risks for head injury, neither the tricycle rider nor any passenger is lawfully required to wear a helmet—again setting a poor expectation for later bicycling.

## HOW LONG WILL IT TAKE?

Using the "pedal magic" technique, Reginald Joules has found that some children—especially those who have never used training wheels—have learned to balance and ride in as little as *five minutes*. John Waterman's more gradual step-by-step program has adults and children with various disabilities bicycling independently within ten weeks, with only one two-hour lesson a week (twenty hours total). However long they take—and this varies widely from child to child—the "BBP No-Fall" and the "pedal magic" techniques are faster than the traditional "Dad" and "downhill" cold-turkey methods, and a lot less terrifying for both parent and child.

Realistically, with daily practice even a cautious child will likely be balancing on two wheels within a week or two, although he or she may be wobbly about starting and stopping. The most important consideration for the child, however, is not speed of learning but achieving a feeling of solid comfort with each skill before going on to the next. Each day you practice, warm up using earlier skills before introducing a new one. If the response to the suggestion of a new experiment is at all hesitant, don't push. Concentrate on solidifying confidence in earlier skills and try new ones at another time.

While this advice to be patient may seem self-evident, it may also be easier said than done in this age of single parenthood and dual-career couples when no one has much time. Many kids need an entire summer of riding an hour or two each day to become proficient. Yet one

*Figure 5-11. Your little one will fall when learning to ride a bicycle, just as when learning to walk. As you did when the child was a toddler, simply soothe the boo-boo, offer a hug, and encourage the child to try again. Note protective gloves on hands.*

overprotective and overcommitted single mom I once knew deprived her twelve-year-old son of learning to ride because he couldn't master it in the couple of mornings she was willing to spend watching him go up and down a one hundred-foot driveway. And she discouraged him from trying on his own. What kind of self-confidence did that inspire in him?

*Remember:* Learning to ride a bike is tricky and scary and takes time to master. That's why virtually all people who ride as adults learned as children, and why exceptionally few people learn to ride once they're adults. When your child falls—and he or she will fall—soothe the boo-boo and send the child back outside, just as you did when the child was learning to walk (see fig. 5-11).

Mastering the elements of braking, balancing, and pedaling is just the beginning. No doubt you knew the theory behind accelerating, steering, and shifting a car months before driving became reflexive. At first you—and your child—do all the operations only with intense concentration of conscious thought. An hour every afternoon riding up and down the sidewalk with neighbor kids can work a marvelous transformation in your child's bike-handling skills in less than a month.

Only when able to handle the bike as comfortably and as unconsciously as he or she handles walking or running should a child graduate to the mental skills of watching for traffic, sightseeing, and dealing with dogs or other surprises. A child who is not in full control of the bike is physically and mentally unprepared to ride while watching for traffic, because part of the mind is always focused on handling the bike itself. One step at a time.

The payoff will be having a wonderful cycling companion in the years to come.

# Chapter 6

# Teaching Traffic Safety to Children

"Traffic safety? What's the big deal? For heaven's sake, a bicycle is a kid's toy!"

*Wrong!* **A bicycle is not a toy; it is a child's first vehicle.**

True, one key reason anyone—adult or child—rides a bicycle is to have fun. People also pilot airplanes, motorboats, automobiles, and motorcycles to have fun. But no one would contest that planes, boats, cars, and motorcycles are vehicles that must be operated in a responsible manner to avoid injury or even death.

Even though a bicycle is not motorized, it does share one essential characteristic with cars and motorcycles: to get anywhere farther than a few blocks from home, the bicycle must be driven in the street, sharing the road with motor vehicles and licensed drivers. If a child is to ride in the street safely, it is imperative that he or she appreciate the dangers of moving vehicles enough to be respectful of them (that is, not to play "chicken"), to anticipate their speed and direction, and to know how to signal turns, to wait at stop signs and lights, and to ride with traffic.

"Geez, that's too much responsibility—just let a kid be a kid. Why take the fun out of it? By the time my kid needs to know that traffic safety stuff, he'll be old enough for driver's ed."

*Wrong again!*

Parents neglecting to teach their children about traffic safety is likely one reason why two-thirds of car-bicycle accidents involve children fifteen and under—primarily due to their not looking while entering roadways, swerving about in the roadway, riding the wrong way, running stop signs, not signaling, or making errors in judging right-of-way. And forty percent of the one thousand or so bicycling fatalities suffered each year in the United States involve children under fourteen.

Some adults use these grim statistics to assert that children on bicycles have no place on the road.

On the contrary, these statistics provide every reason to make sure that children are taught essential traffic laws not only from day 1 on their own bicycles, but from day 0—from the first moment they are put in a child seat or trailer attached to an adult's bike.

Early parental coaching is irreplaceable, because no one else will do it. The century-old nationwide instructional/advocacy organization the League of American Bicyclists (based in Washington, D.C., and known until 1994 as the League of American Wheelmen) holds the view that "parents carry the responsibility of being the child's first bicycle educator." Although since 1995 it has developed courses and videos directed toward children age ten through fifteen, its instructional materials about bicycling with children age four through nine are directed exclusively at parents. Moreover, while there are instructional children's videos on bicycling that illustrate basic bicycling-in-traffic principles, *caveat emptor:* some put out by well-respected safety organizations contain terribly unsafe advice. (For a list of winners and some comments about sinners, see Appendix 3, "Recommended Resources for Parents and Kids.")

Thus, for the first nine years of a child's life, Mom and Dad are the sole source of reliable information on bicycling safety.

## VEHICULAR CYCLING AND BICYCLE "DRIVING"

The most widely recognized authoritative reference on cyclists' sharing the road with motor vehicles is John Forester's *Effective Cycling,* now in its sixth edition (MIT Press, 1993). This six-hundred-page book is widely available at bike shops, in bookstores with good sports/travel sections, and through bicycling-supply mail-order houses.

The fundamental premise of *Effective Cycling* is the principle of vehicular cycling: **"Cyclists fare best when they act and are treated as operators of vehicles."** Key to this concept is the term "bicycle driver." The words are chosen advisedly, to emphasize that an adult or child cyclist is not just a passenger, but the *operator* of a vehicle that happens to have a human motor and two wheels instead of an internal combustion engine and four wheels.

As Forester points out, the purpose of traffic laws is to make traffic behavior predictable. If every driver knows what behavior to follow and to expect, and if every driver actually follows the traffic laws, then traffic accidents will be minimized. In short, driving a vehicle will be as safe as possible.

If a bicycle driver follows the same rules as a motorist, then both people will know what behavior to expect from each other—and there will be fewer accidents. Motorized and nonmotorized vehicles should be able to share the road safely.

Forester's thesis of vehicular-style riding for cyclists has been so compelling that since the 1970s, it has been adopted in the motor vehicle statutes of most states. All state statutes specify that "bicycles," "bicycle drivers," or "operators" have the same rights to the road as motor vehicle drivers—and the same duties to obey traffic laws. In fact, bicycles are explicitly classed as vehicles in many states, including Arkansas, Colorado, Delaware, Florida, Georgia, Iowa, Kentucky, Massachusetts, Minnesota, Missouri, Montana, Nebraska, North Carolina, Ohio, Oregon, Pennsylvania, Texas, Virginia, Washington, and Wisconsin.

That this definition also applies to children's bicycles is clear. An examination of state statutes reveals that some states define a bicycle as a device with wheels larger than 14 inches (Wisconsin) or with a maximum seat height of greater than 25 inches from the ground (Virginia). In other words, bicycles with wheels 16 or 20 inches in diameter—including BMX-style bicycles and bicycles for grade-school children—are regarded as vehicles in the eyes of the law, are legal on roadways, and must follow traffic laws. The statutes also clearly pertain to adults' folding bicycles and recumbent bicycles, many of which use 16- or 20-inch wheels.

The only exceptions are "toy vehicles" or "play vehicles," such as 12-inch children's bicycles, which are expected to be kept on sidewalks.

## CHALLENGES IN TEACHING CHILDREN

Some key physiological and psychological traits of children make teaching traffic safety to them significantly different from teaching it to novice adults.

### Stature and Visibility

The eye level of an adult or child seated on a bicycle is about the same as that of the same person standing. But a grade-schooler commonly has only the eye height of a kneeling adult (see fig. 6-1). While even a short adult may scan over the tops of compact cars, a seven-year-old's eyes are at the same level as those of the car's occupants. Thus, even a watchful child's view of traffic or road hazards will be blocked by the nearest car.

By the same token, a child on a small bicycle is harder for a motorist to see than an adult on a full-sized bicycle.

If you couldn't see a traffic hazard—or be seen yourself—while kneeling in the roadway, your child can't either.

### Reflexes and Control

Not until the teen years do children develop full peripheral vision, fast reflexes, hand-eye coordination, and fine motor control. Even a vigilant seven- or eight-year-old is physically unable to see an approaching car out of the corner of the eye, or to react as quickly as a teen or adult can to get out of danger. Youngsters also don't have the same ability to judge distances or the closing speeds of two vehicles. Nor do they have enough experience in the world to fathom why such abstractions as traffic laws are important.

### Deadly Fantasies

Despite having ridden in cars many times, kids do not necessarily relate to them as inanimate machines piloted by human drivers. Abetted by such favorite fiction as The Little Engine That Could, Theodore the Tugboat, Shining Time Station, and The Magic School Bus, younger children may feel that motor vehicles are live beings whose headlights are big eyes that will look out for them and even rescue them. Unwittingly, adult conversation often reinforces this surrealistic perception. How often have you said something like "I wonder what that car intends to do?" instead of "that driver."

Although older kids may not fall for such "baby stuff," they commonly underestimate the consequences of being hit by a car—after all, how many times have their favorite cartoon superheroes been smashed and emerged unhurt?

*Figure 6-1. A seven-year-old's eye height on a bicycle is about the same as that of a kneeling adult, or of a passenger in a car.*

Emphasize that cars are hunks of iron, piloted by human drivers, that move at speeds that can kill—and that being dead is permanent.

### Styles of Learning

Different children learn best in different ways. Some absorb auditory instructions well, while others must have kinetic, hands-on experience in order to internalize information. A family with more than one child may need to introduce information in a variety of ways for all the children to catch on.

Even the same child may learn in different ways as he or she matures and develops an understanding of cause and effect. Concepts can be reintroduced in increasingly more sophisticated ways at different stages. It is also helpful to reintroduce all basic traffic safety concepts whenever you change environments, such as when moving from a sidewalk or bike path into the street.

Teaching children bicycling traffic safety needs to be an iterative process, incorporating far more review than would be tolerated by a novice adult rider.

## Combating Peer Pressure

For some children in a group of peers, being part of the crowd and having a blast totally eclipse following Mom's or Dad's silly old laws. Besides, the daredevil kid who has a close call with a car and is rewarded with screeching brakes, blaring horn, and shaking fist is a *hero* with a swaggering playground story to tell. In fact, close calls that leave an adult shaken may egg on a kid, especially to the cheers of peers.

One long-term way to ensure your child's safety in a group is to know your child's bicycling friends and coach them in street smarts as well. Encourage your child to invite riding buddies to a local bike rodeo, or take the whole crew out for a day ride—during which you can show all the kids that if they know how to ride in traffic, they can ride really far to cool places.

Children learn far more from consistent example than from words. Reinforce bicycle-safety teachings by two daily practices: correct and lawful behavior in traffic whenever you take your child out bicycling or in the car, and objective analytical commentary assessing other drivers' lawful and unlawful behavior, so your child can learn from the actions of others. On the bicycle, of course, this injunction requires that you change any of your own bad habits, such as drifting through stop signs and red lights, at least when you are with your child. "Do as I say, not as I do" does not work with kids.

## THE UNIFORM VEHICLE CODE

In the United States, the traffic statutes of many states are based on the federal government's Uniform Vehicle Code (UVC). The bicycling sections of the UVC are strongly based on the vehicular principles of Forester's *Effective Cycling*.

For a copy of your state's statutes regarding bicycles, contact the Department of Motor Vehicles or the bicycle/pedestrian coordinator, who is generally in the Department of Transportation in your state's capital. In the absence of access to your own state code, you'll do fine if you follow—and teach your kids to follow—the terms of the Uniform Vehicle Code, which tend to be stricter than the terms of some states.

Below in quotes and italics are simplified sections of the UVC's text (reprinted with permission ©Outdoor Empire Publishing in Seattle, Washington). Each point is followed by an explanation and some suggestions on how to get the point across to kids of various ages.

## Bicyclists Must Obey Traffic Laws

*"Traffic laws apply to persons on bicycles and other human-powered vehicles."*

Emphasize to children that it is a bicycle driver's duty to obey all traffic laws.

Similarly, the bicycle driver has the lawful right to the lanes on all roads, except where bicycles are specifically prohibited, such as on certain limited-access highways, bridges, or tunnels.

Explain rights and duties to grade-school kids by emphasizing how "cars and bicycles need to share the road with each other." This means that both car and bicycle drivers need to "follow the same set of rules (traffic laws and signs) and watch out for one another." They also need to "tell one another what they plan to do" by using signals—flashing-light turn signals in cars and arm signals on bicycles.

Older kids, especially preteens who might be inclined to take their lives into their hands by playing "chicken," also can benefit from a rudimentary lesson in physics: "Is a car hard or soft? Is your body hard or soft? When a big, hard object collides with a small, soft object, which one wins?"

Even children still too young to ride in the street can practice the rules on the sidewalk, to show how grown-up and ready they are for longer bicycle adventures.

## Don't Act Stupid

A number of sections of the UVC specifically outlaw foolhardy behaviors that too often put juveniles at risk, especially once they are big enough to ride on the street.

*"No bicycle can be used to carry more people at one time than the number for which it is designed or equipped."*

This wording was carefully chosen so as to make tandems, child seats, trailercycles, and child trailers legal.

A child should know, however, that it is not legal for one youngster to allow another to hitch a ride by sitting on the handlebars, the top tube, the rear rack, or standing on the foot pegs projecting from the axles of true BMX bicycles. Press your children to give you reasons why such "hitchhiking" is not a good choice. Get them to see various ways it's unsafe for both rider and passenger: it hampers steering, impairs visibility of the road, risks painful impact to the genitalia, and makes the bicycle too top-heavy to remain stable. "And because I love you, I don't want you or your friends to be hurt."

*"No person riding on a bicycle, coaster, roller skates, sled or toy vehicle can attach the vehicle or himself to any other vehicle on a roadway."*

In other words, don't let boys at that age when they feel

# Bicycling with Children

immortal—about ten to fourteen—get a faster thrill by riding a bicycle while holding onto a truck, bus, or other motor vehicle. Seemingly a popular sport in urban areas, it is terrifying to watch, and kids have been killed when they've let go at high speed or when the vehicle has had to make a sudden stop.

If such a hazardous pastime is currently popular in your locale, see if you can arrange to take your preteen to the head-trauma wing of a local hospital to view the lifelong consequences—including irremediable retardation—of potential injury.

*"A person operating a bicycle must keep at least one hand on the handlebars at all times."*

Kids love to ride no-hands.

That may be okay on the school playground, a grassy field, a dirt track, or other place away from motor vehicles where the worst kids can do is fall.

On the roads, however, no cyclist—parent or child—should pull such a stunt. Once the hands are removed from the handlebar, the cyclist must sit straight up to balance. In that position, there is no fast or strong braking—hand brake levers are two feet away out of reach, and there is little leverage for activating a coaster brake with the feet. There is also no possibility of counter-steering, that is, twitching the handlebar to avoid a suddenly seen rock or pothole in the road ahead, or to dodge a barking dog or a car turning right directly in front of the bike.

One-handed operation of the bicycle is legal and is adequate for a short time, in order to signal an upcoming turn, for example, or to take a quick drink from the water bottle.

*"Every bicycle must be equipped with a brake or brakes which will enable its driver to stop the bicycle within 25 feet from a speed of 10 miles per hour on dry, level, clean pavement."*

This section of the Uniform Vehicle Code prohibits the use on roadways of track-racing bikes, which are stripped of all extra weight, including gears and brakes, and are raced on the slanted wooden or concrete track of a velodrome. Brakeless track bikes are often ridden illegally on city streets by urban bicycle messengers, who count on their fast reflexes and agility in steering and dodging to get themselves out of trouble. Such macho weaving in and out of cars, trucks, and buses looks quite dashing to preteen and teenage boys, who perhaps have seen it glorified in such movies as *Quicksilver* and may be inspired to remove the brakes from their own bicycles.

Riding in the roadway without brakes is nothing less than playing Russian roulette on wheels, especially in an area with any kind of hills. You and your kids are smarter than that, right?

Speaking of brakes, it's a good idea periodically to check the braking power of all the family bicycles, to test whether they continue to meet the UVC's standard.

*"A person must not drive a bicycle with earplugs in both ears or while wearing a headset covering both ears."*

Kids, especially preteens and teens, love to listen to the latest groups on headphones.

Fine. Just don't let them listen while on a bicycle.

Teach your child to listen as well as look when riding a bicycle. Children's ears will alert them to motor vehicles approaching from behind; to a dog barking as it streaks across a lawn to nip at their tires; to an overtaking ambulance or fire truck requiring them to pull over to the curb; or of a spoken or shouted warning of a hazard ahead. Parents and kids should also be alert for enjoyable sounds, such as the telltale babble of a hidden waterfall that invites spontaneous exploration—one of the joys of bicycle touring.

Worse than blocking ambient traffic information, earphones from a portable tape or CD player also split the cyclist's attention between the road and the music. A child usually has trouble enough focusing on the complexities of bicycling in traffic without an additional distraction.

Note that the UVC's wording makes it legal to bicycle while wearing hearing aids and one-eared communication systems, such as a walkie-talkie for keeping track of a group ride.

*"If conditions warrant, a uniformed police officer may require the cyclist to stop and submit the bicycle to an inspection."*

If a police officer suspects that your or your child's bicycle is unsafe or stolen, that officer has the right under law to ask you to stop in order to inspect the bicycle.

### Go with the (Traffic) Flow

The part of the Uniform Vehicle Code dealing with riding in the roadway has different ramifications for children of different ages and abilities, and requires substantial discussion.

*"Anyone operating a bicycle on a roadway at less than the normal speed of traffic must ride as close as practicable to the right-hand curb or edge of the roadway, except:*

   **a.** *when overtaking and passing another bicycle or vehicle proceeding in the same direction.*

**b.** *when preparing for a left turn at an intersection or into a private road or driveway.*

**c.** *when reasonably necessary to avoid conditions, such as a substandard width lane, that make it unsafe to continue along the right hand curb or edge."*

Emphasize to kids that "because bicycles are vehicles, bicycles in the street must ride in the same direction as cars. That is called 'riding with the flow of traffic.'" As with a car, a bicycle driver's position in the lanes should be determined by both speed and intent. Usually cyclists travel more slowly than motorists, so generally they should stay near the right in the right-hand lane.

*Note:* Riding to the right with the flow of traffic directly contradicts the bicycling instruction older parents or younger grandparents may have received in their youth. In the 1950s and 1960s, the received wisdom was that bicycles should be ridden on the left-hand side of the road facing traffic, similar to pedestrians walking alongside a roadway having no sidewalks.

The UVC recognizes that riding against the traffic is one of the most dangerous things a cyclist can do. In fact, a quarter to a third of all bike-car accidents happen as a direct result of wrong-way riding. To older kids, you can explain the physics of how the respective speeds of an opposing bicycle and car are added rather than subtracted. To make sure they understand, have the kids calculate the impact. If a car driven at 25 mph overtakes a bicycle being pedaled with traffic at 10 mph, the two have a closing speed of 15 mph (25 - 10); but if the bicycle is being ridden against traffic, the closing speed is 35 mph (25 + 10), and a head-on collision may be fatal.

Younger children may find the concept of riding to the right surprisingly hard to comprehend. Even grade-school children often have trouble telling right from left. More subtly, some children who are able to identify left from right still have trouble understanding that left and right are relative instead of absolute directions. After all, when they exit the front door of their house, don't they always turn left to walk to school?

If the child does not comprehend right and left as relative directions, you'll know this after one ride the length of a sidewalk, bike path, or street. Your child may readily ride down the street on the right-hand side with traffic, but when you turn around at the end to retrace your route, the child instinctively will want to ride back on the same side, that is, on the left side facing traffic. In this instance, the child is attaching the direction "right" to that particular side of the street, much as adults identify the "east" side of the street.

*The solution:* Explain to all children from the outset that the right side of the sidewalk, bike path, or street *is the side closest to their right hand when they are facing the direction they wish to head.* When they turn around to return, the right side of the street will be the side opposite to that ridden on the outbound trip.

If a child is hesitant or confused, before each ride put a sticker or draw a big R on the back of the right hand. Then ask the children always to ride on the side of the sidewalk, bike path, or street closest to the sticker or R. *Note:* Don't assume that your little one necessarily knows the meaning of *curb, gutter, driveway, asphalt, drainage grate,* or other common roadway terms.

Children must internalize into reflex the knowledge that, for traffic flow, *right and left are relative to their bodies and **not** to the landscape.* Why? In most cases moving right means moving toward greater safety while moving left means moving into traffic—and on a return route, you do not want a simple misunderstanding to cause your beloved child to move into, instead of away from, the path of danger.

When your kids grow old enough to understand that traffic laws sometimes require judgment of degree, introduce some of the complexities required in judging how far to the right is "practicable."

The UVC explicitly recognizes three specific circumstances when a cyclist should not ride to the far right: when passing a slower moving entity such as another cyclist, a jogger, etc.; when positioning yourself to turn left from a left-turn lane, as the driver of a car would do (left turns are discussed in another section below); and when riding far to the right is hazardous.

Especially on narrow, shoulderless roads or bridges, many experienced cyclists advise riding about a third of the way to the left— about where the passenger sits in a car or where the right front tire tracks. This position will force cars approaching from behind to slow down and move left a bit to pass you. The object of claiming this much of the lane is to prevent you and your kids from being squeezed off the right-hand edge of the road.

Even on roads with lanes of standard width, the words "as far right as practicable" do *not* mean clinging to the far right-hand edge. First, the gutter or pavement's edge may be broken, littered with gravel, sand, or broken glass, or punctuated with drains with tire-eating slots—all of which you and your family will miss if you're riding a few feet to the left. Second, motorists may not notice a cyclist riding to the far right, because they do not expect to see a vehicle moving at the curb or shoulder unless it is slowing down to stop. If you're too far right, cars tend to blow right by you and cut you off when they turn right. Third, if you're a few feet to the left, an overtaking driver will have to slow down and move around you to the left. As that may involve his encroachment into the lane for oncoming traffic, he is likely to pass you with more care than if he feels you are so far to the right that he could whiz by without swerving.

When passing parked cars, teach kids to ride two or three feet to their left, out of range of a suddenly opening door. Also teach them to look for a driver's silhouette inside the car, exhaust being emitted from the tailpipe, or a front wheel turned left—all indications that the driver intends to pull out of the parking place. Warn youngsters never to pass on the right-hand side of a taxi or bus that has stopped midlane to discharge passengers; that is tantamount to asking to be "doored" or to collide with a pedestrian.

Teach older kids to *ride a straight line* whenever possible. Driving a bicycle in a straight line keeps a cyclist visible and predictable, and is expected vehicular behavior—exactly what motorists do. Don't duck to the right (i.e., closer to the curb) on long stretches between parked cars; continue to ride straight as if all the parking spaces were occupied and doors were opening (see fig. 6-2).

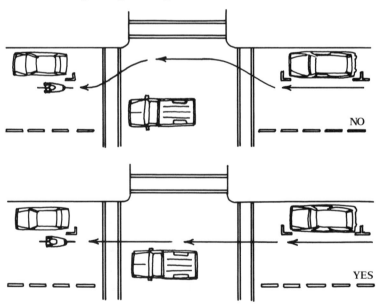

*Figure 6-2. Teach kids to ride a straight line and not duck to the right in empty spaces between cars or at intersections.*

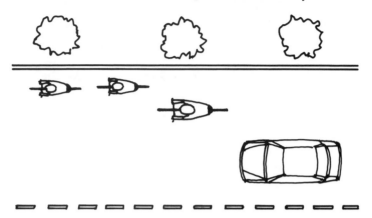

*Figure 6-3. A parent should ride behind and slightly to the left of children.*

To adult novice cyclists, all this lane-claiming may seem to be deliberately putting yourself into the path of cars. On the contrary, lane-claiming is part of predictable vehicular behavior, which most motorists recognize—and it is also recognized by law.

Best of all, it really, truly works. Try it. And teach your kids.

### Ride Single File

*"People riding bicycles on a roadway must not ride more than two abreast except on paths or parts of roadways set aside for the exclusive use of bicycles."*

In general, children riding on their own bicycles should ride in front of an adult. If you're out with one or more other parents, have the kids ride single-file between the adults, with the most experienced adult riding "sweep" in the rear. This is a family version of the "point, sweep, and drop" system followed for safety by commercial tour organizations (for more details on this system, see Chapter 7, "Family and Group Rides: Where to Go, What to Take"). As sweep, you can easily keep an eye on your kids, coaching them and warning them of cars approaching from behind.

On little-traveled rural roads, you and your child may ride side by side as long as there is no traffic. When riding abreast, the parent—who is the more experienced rider—should ride to the left of the child. As soon as you see a motor vehicle overtaking you in your rearview mirror, reposition your bicycle so that you are riding behind but still slightly to the left of your child (see fig 6-3). This way a passing car must give wider berth to the child. Moreover, even if the child veers a little left or falls, your position shields him or her from overtaking traffic.

### Left Turns for Younger and Older Children

The UVC allows a cyclist two options for making a left turn: turning in the same manner as a motor vehicle, or turning almost like a pedestrian.

   **a**. *"A person riding a bicycle must use the turn in the extreme left-hand lane lawfully available to traffic for that purpose.*

   **b**. *Or, a person riding a bicycle must approach the turn as close as practicable to the right curb or edge of the roadway. After proceeding across the intersection to the far corner, the bicyclist must stop out of the way of traffic. The bicyclist must yield to any traffic and obey all traffic control devices before proceeding in the new direction.*

   *A right or left turn signal must be given not less than the last 100 feet traveled before turning, and must be given while the bicyclist is stopped, waiting to turn."*

When turning left pedestrian-style, the bicycle driver stays on the right-hand side of the road and rides all the way across the intersection. On the opposite side, he or she then waits for the cross-traffic light to turn green. Once the motor vehicles already in line have driven off, the bicycle driver then follows in the new direction (see fig. 6-4). This pedestrian-style left turn is preferred for parents escorting independently riding children who are as yet too inexperienced to judge the closing speed of overtaking traffic.

   *Note:* Cyclists must not drive their bicycles in the crosswalk. If you and your kids wish to turn left using the crosswalk, dismount and walk your bicycles across the street as actual pedestrians.

   When turning left in the manner of a motor vehicle, the bicycle driver has the lawful right to merge as far left as possible—into the dedicated left turn lane, if such exists. In fact, the cyclist should behave exactly as if he or she were driving a car: signaling left; scanning, that is, looking back, to see that the next lane left is clear; moving into the next lane; scanning again; and moving into the left turn lane to make the turn. There the bicycle driver either waits for the left turn

*Figure 6-4. Younger children should turn left almost as if they were pedestrians (top)—or should dismount and cross as actual pedestrians (bottom).*

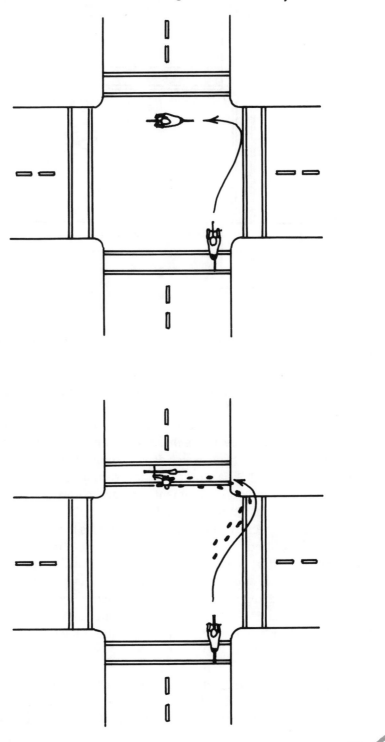

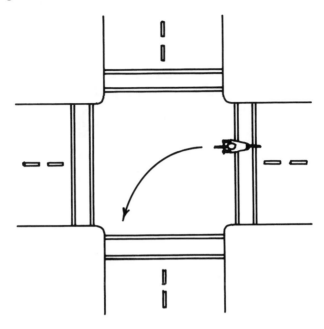

*Figure 6-5. Teens competent to ride in traffic may turn left as if they were driving a motor vehicle.*

arrow or, if there is none, yields to oncoming traffic before completing the left turn (see fig. 6-5).

The motor vehicle-style left turn requires that if several cyclists are traveling together, *each one merges independently,* **not** *as a group,* just as automobile drivers do even if driving somewhere together in separate cars. Turning left like a motor vehicle is recommended only for teens with fast reflexes and good judgment, who are mature enough to take a driver education class in high school.

A word needs to be said about arm signals for cyclists. In all fifty states, the recognized three signals for left turn, right turn, and stopping are all performed by the left arm: straight out for a left turn, pointing down for stopping, and pointing up for a right turn. A few states' statutes also legally allow the right arm to be used to indicate a right turn (see fig. 6-6). Even if your state allows that alternative, teach your kids the proper left-arm signal for a right turn—they may need it on an out-of-state bicycle vacation.

*Figure 6-6. Standard arm signals for left turn (A), stopping (B), and right turn (C) are recognized in all fifty states. Some states statutes also allow cyclists to use the right arm (D) as a legal alternative to indicate a right turn.*

### Breaking a Tie

*"When two vehicles approach or enter an intersection from different highways at approximately the same time, the driver of the vehicle on the left must yield the right-of-way to the vehicle on the right."*

This is the same rule that motorists follow when motor vehicles simultaneously approach a four-way stop from different roads. Depending exclusively upon the vehicles' relative positions, sometimes the bicycle driver yields to the car driver; sometimes the car driver yields to the bicycle driver. Once again, to understand who goes first, the child must know that the direction "right" is with respect to the cyclist's own body (see fig. 6-7).

### Sidewalks and Crosswalks

*"A person using a bicycle on a sidewalk or in a crosswalk must yield the right-of-way to any pedestrian, and must give an audible signal before overtaking and passing any pedestrians."*

Teach children that when riding their bicycles on the sidewalk, they must give priority to people walking or jogging. If they want to pass a pedestrian, they need to give a polite verbal warning—even a simple "excuse me" is effective.

*Avoid* using the athlete's common shorthand "on your left," meaning that you are passing on the left; half the time, nonathletic pedestrians will interpret the words as a command to move to the left, directly into the cyclist's path. You and your kids will usually get a better response by slowing down enough to be more explicit: "Hello, I'm coming up on your left."

Make sure to instruct kids to wait until they see the person move before trying to pass; some pedestrians may be hard of hearing, infirm, or simply preoccupied with their own thoughts.

Remember to teach your kids to add a courteous "thank you!" as they ride past.

### Bells and Whistles

*"A bicycle must not be equipped with any siren or whistle. Bicyclists must not use sirens or whistles."*

Do not let your child signal his or her presence on a bicycle by blowing a police whistle. Doing so is actually illegal, because it could be construed as impersonating an officer.

Figure 6-7. (A) At a four-way stop, this bicycle driver should let the motorist proceed first; (B) this automobile driver should let the cyclist proceed first.

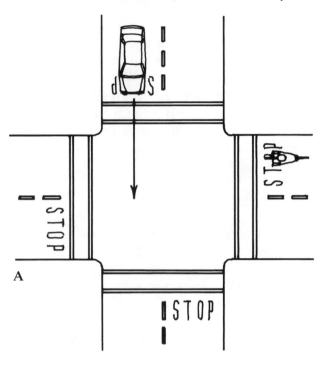

A

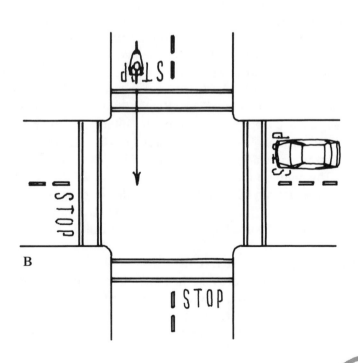

B

A bicycle bell is required by the traffic statutes of many states—and is a good idea even if it isn't. Most pedestrians respond favorably to a bicycle bell, recognizing what it is and glancing around to see where the bicycle is before stepping aside.

Bells are somewhat safer for kids than air horns. A bell's lever can be triggered by a thumb instead of requiring a child to take the whole hand off the handlebar to squeeze the horn's rubber bulb. *Tip:* For a youngster riding in the street, make sure to buy the loudest bell possible.

### Be Visible After Dark

*"Every vehicle on a highway from a half hour after sunset to a half hour before sunrise must emit a white light visible from a distance of at least 500 feet to the front. A red rear reflector must be visible for 600 feet to the rear.*

*"Every bicycle must be equipped with reflective material to be visible from both sides for 600 feet."*

True, the best prevention is not to let younger kids ride in the street after dark. And that is the advice most commonly found in safety booklets concerning children and bicycling: don't do it.

For kids of twelve or fourteen, however, such advice is neither informative nor helpful. After the onset of standard time, depending on both your latitude and your east-west position in your time zone, twilight may begin even earlier than 4:00 P.M. and linger past 8:00 A.M. Those are times when middle school, junior-high, or high school students may be bicycling to or from sports practice, music lessons, or a part-time job.

According to the UVC, a bicycle needs not only reflectors, but also a headlight that emits a white light visible to motorists and pedestrians at least 500 feet from the front. This minimum requirement is satisfied by most inexpensive or moderately priced battery-operated or generator-driven headlights available in a bicycle shop.

This minimum requirement set by the UVC, however, may not be enough, especially in areas without bright street lights. Lighting systems appropriate for teens who will be riding in twilight or darkness are discussed more fully in Chapter 8, "An Ounce of Prevention . . . "

## FORESTER'S FIVE PRINCIPLES

According to John Forester, the fundamentals of bicycling in traffic, whether or not codified in law, can be distilled down to five basic principles. If you can get these five principles across, even a younger child will be eighty percent of the way toward avoiding traffic conflicts. Teens should be encouraged to read Forester's *Effective Cycling* for them-selves—they will enjoy his "in your face" writing style.

Four of Forester's five principles are rules dealing with inter-sections. Even very young children should practice the first two basic principles while they are riding on the sidewalk. They'll have plenty of opportunity and need—and will be more ready when it's time to gradu-ate to driving their bicycles in the street.

**1**. *Drive with traffic on the right-hand side of a sidewalk, bike path, or street.*
Remember that "traffic" means not only motor vehicles, but also pedestrians on sidewalks and cyclists, skateboarders, inline skaters, joggers, and others who happen to be using a bike path or roadway.

**2**. *When reaching a more important or larger road than the one you are on, yield to crossing traffic—that is, look to both sides and wait until the way ahead is clear.*
Yielding to larger streets is one of the most essential principles of traffic safety for young children to learn. The single leading cause of car-bike accidents involving children under age ten has to do with their not looking for cross traffic before coasting out of a driveway into the street. Moreover, if a child riding on a sidewalk wants to cross a street, he or she must be especially vigilant; even a driver stopped at a stop sign at the intersection may not necessarily see the child, as motorists rarely look for traffic on sidewalks.
Explain that an intersection is where one road crosses another. Each driveway to a house, for example, forms an intersection with the sidewalk where a child must be vigilant about crossing traffic. Motorists exiting or entering their driveways are sup-posed to yield to pedestrians on the sidewalk, but often they do not. Similarly, each place where a bike path crosses a driveway or service road is also an intersection.
Emphasize also that *not every intersection where a cyclist must yield is marked by a yield sign, stop sign, or traffic light*. Bicyclists and other vehicle drivers simply are expected to know that wider, more important roads have the right-of-way—that is, that traffic on the wider road has the right to keep going at full speed.
School your children in the proper way to yield to cross traffic

when exiting a driveway, especially if they intend to cross the road or turn left.

First, make sure that the child is standing at the ready in the "power position": both hands should be on the handlebars and one pedal should be up under the power foot, poised to be pushed instantly for a quick scoot across the street (see fig. 6-8). The child should *not* be standing with both feet on the ground, as traffic patterns can change in the moments lost while fumbling for the pedals.

Next, the child must really *look* for traffic, not just mindlessly turn the head. The child should first look left, then right—and then left again—to spot anyone who may have sneaked out of a driveway during the moment the child was looking right. Emphasize the importance of waiting until no approaching car is in sight, or is at least a block away; use your judgment for the specific configuration and traffic speed of your local streets. When both lanes are clear of approaching traffic for at least a block in both directions, the child should cross the street as quickly as is safe.

Last, if several kids are riding together, emphasize that each child must make his or her *independent* decision about the right time to cross the street—they should not just "follow the leader." Following the leader is, in fact, highly dangerous, as traffic patterns can change drastically in moments.

As tempting as it is for a parent, try not to do the looking and deciding for your kids and shout "all clear!" Instead, coach each beginner individually: "Okay, look left—see any cars or other traffic closer than a block away? No? Look right—see anything? No? Quickly check left again. What do you think? Good decision—*go!*"

If possible, let older, experienced kids coach younger siblings. Not only do younger kids often listen better to older kids than to their parents, but the act of teaching proper techniques can reinforce the knowledge for the older kids and make them feel more responsible. Award verbal stars to children for making their own decisions, and give reminders or demerits when kids blithely follow parents or other kids without looking.

*Figure 6-8. A child yielding to cross traffic should have pedal up under the power foot, ready to roll, and then look to the left (1), the right (2), and the left again (3) before proceeding across the street.*

Forester's other three principles regarding bicycling in traffic pertain primarily to preteens or teens competent enough to drive their bicycles regularly in the street.

3. *When changing lanes, yield to traffic in the new lane—that is, look forward and backward until you see that the way is clear.*

    This principle is essential for positioning the bicycle to turn left from a left turn lane, as a motor vehicle would.

    Instruct your child that simply sticking out the left arm to signal a turn is not sufficient. The child must also *learn to scan.* The trick here is to keep the bicycle heading straight while glancing backward, a skill at which children as young as six or seven are quite adept.

    Encourage a child to practice scanning on a sidewalk or at a playground with a game called "Who's There?" which is popular at bicycle safety rodeos. Stand in one spot while your child rides away from you; when you call out "now!" instruct the child to look back over a shoulder and tell you how many fingers you have raised on one hand (see fig. 6-9). Repeat the game as often as necessary until the child can ride a straight line without wobbling or veering when turning the head. If the child has trouble turning the head far enough, suggest that he or she drop that shoulder while looking backward.

*Figure 6-9. Have a child practice scanning for traffic by keeping the bicycle heading straight while looking back over a shoulder to identify the number of fingers held up by an adult or friend.*

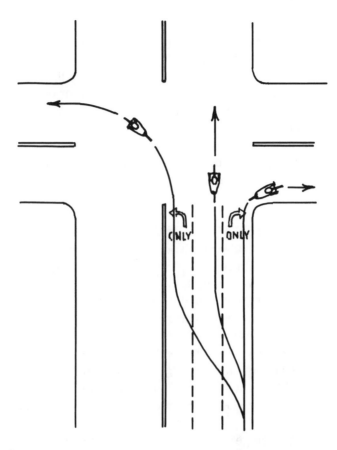

*Figure 6-10. Teen and adult cyclists should position themselves in the lane depending both on their speed relative to other traffic and on their intended destination.*

4. *When approaching an intersection, position the bicycle with respect to the direction of your destination: toward the centerline for a left turn, toward the curb for a right turn, and between the two for continuing straight.*

   This is nothing more or less than what any motorist does. Your position, plus arm signals, communicates your intentions to other drivers (see fig. 6-10).

5. *Between intersections, position yourself with respect to your speed relative to the rest of traffic.*

   Slower traffic should be traveling nearer the curb, faster traffic should be nearer the centerline.

Where the bicycle driver's speed matches that of the automobile traffic—such as on fast downhills—cyclists have the *lawful right* to move left into the flow of traffic to claim the entire lane. Moreover, where the cars slow down to match the cyclist's speed, such as when approaching a stop sign or red light, cyclists again should move left to take their proper turn in the order of traffic.

*Note:* When approaching a stop light, kids and parents should not coast past the line of waiting cars to go to the front of the line, any more than motorists should cut ahead by driving on the road's shoulder.

## TEACH BICYCLE TRAFFIC LAWS FROM INFANCY

How early should children be exposed to the concepts of traffic safety?

Children should be taught traffic laws and bicycling etiquette literally from infancy or toddlerhood—even before they learn to ride a bicycle on their own. This acquaints and accustoms them to the existence of safety rules for bicycles and cars.

It's easy and fun!

Even before a child can read, a bicycling parent with a child passenger can point out that the big red sign with the big white letters means "Stop!" "And what do we do at a stop sign?" you ask. "Stop!" shouts the child. And so you do, putting your foot down on the pavement, to the child's glee. "Okay, look left. Do you see any cars? I don't. How about to the right? None? Look left again. Is it safe for us to go? What a good traffic director you are!" Over and over again, ride after ride, you play this game together.

Preschoolers, who are naturally curious about all they see, can be taught to be alert to a remarkable number of road markings and traffic signs. An added advantage is that many traffic warning signs are designed to be understood without words. While on the bike together, quiz your young passenger about the meaning of each yellow warning sign, demonstrating the meaning as the opportunity allows: "What does that big arrow mean? Yep, a right-hand turn ahead. And he-e-ere we go—lean right!"

Alternate this game with one in which you assign the child the duty of looking for potholes, dangerous sewer grates, broken glass, piles of leaves, and other road hazards. Soon, your three- or four-year-old may be spotting hazards before you do—thereby learning vigilance about what is important in road conditions.

You can also train a preschooler in the etiquette of signaling intentions to other drivers on the road. By encouraging mimicry, you may soon find junior imitating your turn signals, looking back before changing lanes, and echoing your call of "car back!" to riding companions. In short, the child is no longer a passenger, but a copilot.

Even when behind the wheel of a car, you can continue bicycle traffic instruction. Some bicycling parents play a game called "What Will That Car Do Next?" in which, based upon a car's position and signaling, the child tries to deduce what the driver will do. In addition to making a long drive more interesting for children, this game teaches them how to be observant about moving traffic and the intentions of drivers.

Also in the car, continue the reinforcement of watching for traffic signs by playing a traffic-safety variation of "I Spy." Hand youngsters crayons and photocopies of the road signs from the traffic law booklet from your state's Department of Motor Vehicles and challenge them to be first to circle the various signs they see. Older children can vie to be the first to shout out their meanings as well.

## FROM SIDEWALK TO STREET: AT WHAT AGE?

There is no fixed age at which it is recommended or legal for child bicyclists to graduate from sidewalk to street. Most child-safety coloring books recommend that children stick to the sidewalks through age eight. The League of American Bicyclists constructs its Kids II course to teach children ages ten through twelve the skills necessary for driving their bicycles on lightly traveled residential streets. On the other hand, in some rural communities without sidewalks, children as young as five or six bicycle on the roadways. Use your judgment, based on the configuration and traffic patterns of streets in your neighborhood.

Ideal for tots venturing on the roadway for the first time are the streets of a retirement community, as they are usually level and posted at 10 or 15 mph to accommodate wheelchairs and walkers. Alternatively, try a paved road blocked to motorists at certain times of the day, the roads around an RV campground or trailer park, or the lightly traveled streets of a cul-de-sac residential community. A paved bicycle path will also serve, if you pretend that other users are buses and cars and other motor vehicles.

Once they graduate to the street, encourage children to practice all the traffic laws they know. This will be surprisingly tough—there are so many distractions in the new environment that even well-trained grade-schoolers may act as if they've forgotten two years of reinforcement.

Last, make the *privilege* of riding in the street contingent upon their learning correct habits. Withdraw the privilege for a week if you learn they lapse into careless and dangerous riding; either ground them altogether, or confine them to the sidewalk with the "little kids"—the humiliation alone will likely bring them into line.

Teaching grade-schoolers safe bicycling provides the opportunity to build a foundation in *not only the skills but also the reflexes* needed to be safe. Your children will be ready to be responsible motor vehicle drivers by the time they are old enough to terrify you by asking for the car keys. By the time he or she has a learner's permit, a teen schooled in sound bicycling traffic principles will already be a seasoned vehicular driver with some ten years of experience, not merely the statutory six months the permit requires before a license is awarded.

Given the statistical rate of traffic accidents claiming the lives of inexperienced teen motorists, that alone should be a comfort—and reason enough to start early in childhood to teach a child vehicular bicycle driving.

# Chapter 7

# Family and Group Rides: Where to Go, What to Take

Half-day and daylong bicycle rides are great fun for all ages. Even a restless toddler who normally does not like sitting still will stop squirming when the bike starts to move and the scenery speeds by.

To the extent possible, depending on their age, *involve the kids in planning the routes and destinations*—not only to give them some planning experience and sense of geography, but also to make the outing their ride, not just the parents' "crummy old trip."

## HOW LONG A TRIP TO PLAN

Conservatively, by age seven any active, healthy child will be able to mosey along a flat route and cover 10 to 20 miles in a day. As that range is also conservative for parents unaccustomed to bicycling, the family should be evenly matched. Seven-year-olds of avid cyclists have been known to ride as far as 35 to 50 miles in a day, and still have energy for the playground in the afternoon. No, they're not junior Olympic champions—a good bicycle is an extraordinarily efficient machine that makes riding easy.

If a parent is severely out of shape or if one child is as young as four, a safe introductory bike tour is 3 to 5 miles long. If the child wants to stop and explore every 50 feet, such a short ride will take two or three hours. And if the child wants to play speed demon, well, you can always do the route twice.

The most important result you want from the first-ever family ride is that everyone reaches the end feeling great!

## WHERE TO GO

Half a day or a whole day on a bicycle is a long time to a little one. *Pick routes having many stops attractive to children.* The best destinations are simple places, such as a small museum, a lighthouse, a bird blind, a working farm open to visitors, or even an unfamiliar playground. And, of course, a picnic lunch is always a hit.

Until you and your children are all equipped with derailleur bicycles and are experienced in using the low gears, *keep the route as flat as possible.* The smaller wheels of kids' bicycles require their young riders to pedal furiously to attain any kind of speed. Their wide, low-pressure tires have a lot of rolling resistance. Made of cheaper steel, kids' bikes commonly weigh 25 pounds—as much as an adult's bike, and up to fully half the child's weight. For comparison, think how much work it is for you to pedal your bicycle loaded with an additional 50 pounds. Despite those equipment handicaps, many 16- and 20-inch bikes have no low gears to help their young riders up hills—and their single gear is the equivalent of one of your *high* gears. If you would be happy pedaling the route on a heavy one-speed cruiser, your kids will do fine also.

Once your family's fitness increases and all members are skilled in operating the gears of their derailleur bicycles, flat routes will begin to seem boring. Moreover, in many areas few flat routes are available, so being able to tackle some rolling terrain will expand the variety of scenery and fun destinations. (For teaching kids how to use low gears to make hill-climbing a cinch, see Chapter 5, "Learning to Ride: Ready, Set, Balance!")

Depending on your kids' levels of maturity, *choose routes carefully for their motor vehicle traffic.* Where kindergartners and young grade-schoolers are to ride their own bicycles, you'll want a route essentially free from motor vehicles. Older children and preteens can gain valuable traffic-handling practice on lightly traveled roads. Adolescents may be skilled enough to ride on any roads attractive to adult cyclists.

### Bike Paths, Towpaths, Rail Trails

Your first choice for a route closed to motor vehicles may be the paved multiuse paths provided by many cities.

Surprise, surprise: on a sunny Saturday or Sunday, paved paths will also attract inline skaters (who often take over the whole path as they sway from side to side), dog-walkers, joggers with baby strollers, and other families on bicycles—in other words, a sometimes daunting volume of nonmotorized traffic. The constantly moving crowd can be distressing to a youngster still feeling wobbly (see fig. 7-1).

*Figure 7-1. Paved bicycle paths can have enough traffic volume to disturb small children on their bicycles.*

# Bicycling with Children

Often solitude can be gained by riding on unpaved canal towpaths, aqueduct trails, and rail trails (see fig. 7-2). Their surfaces are usually hard-packed dirt or crushed gravel, both fine for any type of bicycle, especially a few days after a rain, when the surface is tamped firm and dust-free. Because the trails follow waterways and railroad corridors, they seldom have a grade steeper than a few percent. In fact, if ridden in the correct direction, the whole route can be a gentle downhill! As the single trail is well defined, kids can't get lost, and older ones are able to enjoy a bit of independence in riding ahead and then doubling back to meet up with slower siblings.

Canal towpaths were originally constructed in the eastern and midwestern United States in the nineteenth century as walkways for mules and horses pulling barges along a canal. County maps or the series of topographic state atlases and gazetteers published by the DeLorme Company (widely available at bookstores with good travel departments) will map out any canals in your area, and may even show whether they have towpaths accessible to bicycles. A local bike shop or canal museum may also have more detailed maps.

In a few regions, such as Westchester County, New York, you may find aqueduct trails: dirt trails that are public easements running atop a course of aqueducts carrying drinking water from a reservoir to a city. Aqueduct trails are seldom widely known outside the immediate vicinity. If you live within a reasonable distance of a reservoir serving a major city, ask a local bike shop if an aqueduct trail exists, or examine a detailed county or topographic map to determine this for yourself.

Rail trails are former railroad corridors converted into eight- to twelve-foot-wide multiuse paths that never exceed a gentle grade, allowing easy access even for children and wheelchairs. Individual rail trails range in length from half a mile to hundreds of miles, and can be found in forty-eight of the fifty states (there are none in Delaware or Hawaii). Some one thousand abandoned railroad beds totaling more than ten thousand miles have been preserved for recreational cyclists, thanks mainly to the efforts of both local activists and the nonprofit organization Rails-to-Trails Conservancy, based in Washington, D.C. (See Appendix 3, "Recommended Resources for Parents and Kids," for detailed guides to towpaths, aqueduct trails, and rail trails.)

*Figure 7-2. Unpaved canal towpaths, aqueduct trails, and rail trails are ideal for family bicycling.*

## *Light-Traffic Roads*

Little-traveled residential or rural roads make for excellent family riding with children practicing basic traffic-handling skills (see fig. 7-3). Paved farm roads are ideal: they are usually long, flat, and straight, so that overtaking or approaching motor vehicles are visible from a mile away, and traffic volume is commonly less than one vehicle per minute. *Note:* Some state transportation departments publish maps that rate roads by their traffic volume, a great tool for planning family outings.

Forested routes are pretty, but they may not be suitable for younger riders. As forests are commonly at higher elevations, the roads tend to be curvy—giving less line-of-sight warning of approaching cars—and rolling—requiring more bike- and traffic-handling skills on downhill curves ending at stop signs. Save these routes for preteens or teens with experienced reflexes.

## *Ride Guidebooks and How to Use Them*

Unfortunately, as yet no series of guidebooks exists for bicycle tours specifically for children. The one guide available for any part of the United States is about Washington, D.C. However, you can get ideas for kid-friendly routes by reading the ride descriptions in bicycle route guidebooks specifically intended for novices.

When you're out enjoying the scenery along a route published in a guidebook, it is easy to bypass your next turn or miss a site you wish to visit, so *take a recently printed county map* along with you. County maps are found in many bookstores, stationery shops, and corner newsstands, in addition to specialty map and travel stores.

Moreover, before hitting the road, spend a few minutes *familiarizing the whole family with the route.* Compare the route map in a book with the description of turns, and compare both with the county map—especially if the guidebook is several years old. Underline or highlight directions in the narrative as well as any attraction you wish to see. Annotate and highlight both the book's route map and the county map, noting landmarks—parks, churches, etc.—and marking turns. Note which intersections are T (where the road you are on dead-ends at another and you must go either right or left) or Y (where the road you are on splits into two at a fork).

Also note very long or very short mileages. If you don't have an

*Figure 7-3. Flat, straight farm roads are great for allowing children to practice traffic-awareness skills.*

odometer, use your watch. As most sight-seeing novice touring cyclists tool along level ground at about 6 or 8 miles per hour—which is also a good sedate speed for children on their own bicycles—a mile takes seven to ten minutes to ride. If you have a 3-mile level stretch without turns in front of you, you know you can relax for a good twenty minutes before having to worry about looking for the next turn.

*Be aware:* Maps themselves have errors. Moreover, new construction can suddenly start in undeveloped scenic areas, and thus may not appear on either the map or in the guidebook. In such cases, ask a local resident about an alternate route.

## WHAT TO TAKE

Chapter 8, "An Ounce of Prevention," details the ten emergency items it's advisable to take on every day or multiday ride—water, fruit and salty snacks, tool kit, maintenance medications and supplies, first-aid kit, extra shirts, medical insurance cards, pencil and paper, bungee cords and a few safety pins, and sunscreen. In addition to these necessities, don't forget fun items such as swimsuits and water sandals, towels, picnic lunch, and a long novel.

In each day's lunch, pack plenty of complex carbohydrates for instant energy: sandwiches of whole-grained bread with plenty of lettuce and tomato and sprouts, carrot sticks, yogurt, fresh and dried fruit. Experienced cyclists especially like bananas; not only are they an excellent source of nutrition and energy, but they also are high in potassium and therefore help restore electrolytes lost through sweating. Avoid fatty foods such as mayonnaise, potato chips, or french fries, which are hard to digest and make you feel sluggish. And pack more food than you think you will possibly need—you and your kids will eat more than you expect.

Pack plenty of water and fruit juices. Juice boxes, if frozen overnight, will keep a lunch cool until midday, and by then will be thawed but still refreshingly chilled.

## RELAX FOR FAMILY HAPPINESS

How can parents and children of differing abilities best enjoy each other's company on the road?

First, *never allow siblings to make the difference in strengths an issue of competition in self-worth.* Let the youngest and weakest children set the pace, with teens and parents keeping an eye on them from the rear. At lunch, older kids who are chomping at the bit can go off for a fast-paced solo circuit. Or, if they are using a guidebook and following a route that shows a longer and a shorter option, the family might even split accordingly and meet later.

If you have two kids of widely differing abilities, let each invite a buddy along. Each pair can do the ride at a different pace, without the slower child feeling left in the dust by the stronger sibling. If younger riders or passengers become tired and cranky, distract them with songs, snacks, and games. Encourage older kids to carry extra gear or take a plastic bag for picking up litter along the way. The extra weight or time for the task will even out the riding speeds. Compliment all kids often on their accomplishments, and reward them at the end of the ride with a healthful treat.

## MULTIDAY FAMILY INN-TO-INN TOURS

If the family enjoys day rides, why not try some bigger adventures, such as a weekend or weeklong bicycle vacation? There are three basic categories of bicycle tours: commercial touring, credit card touring, and independent loaded touring (bike camping). The first two are varieties of inn-to-inn tours.

*Commercial bicycle touring* is similar to taking a cruise. You and your family prepay for a trip offered by a commercial bicycle-touring outfit, and then show up at the right place on the appointed day. Commonly the overnights are at picturesque bed-and-breakfast inns offering gourmet cuisine. Some also offer group camping tours or off-road mountain biking tours, which range from being rustic to posh.

Many commercial tour organizations rank rides by grade of difficulty, even suggesting different routes on the same trip for family members of different ambitions. Trips range in length from one day to several months. In all cases, the organization has mapped the itinerary, planned for overnight stays, and arranged most if not all meals—and it may also offer bicycles and helmets for rent. Commercial tours are also often trailed by a "sag wagon," a van or truck that carries the guests' luggage, picks up weary riders, if necessary, and whose driver is an experienced bike mechanic who can fix breakdowns. You need carry nothing on your bicycles but a water bottle, snacks, and camera.

Commercial bicycle tours are a low-risk way to explore bicycling vacations—although you never know what your family's chemistry might be with the other guests in the group. Few commercial outfits offer tours designed for families alone, although quite a number accept child cyclists, especially adolescents over age twelve. Some offer tours specifically for women, which may be attractive to mothers and daughters, although a disproportionate share of the guests on commercial tours tend to be women anyway.

For families who do not wish to ride as part of a tour group but still want their routes mapped, overnight reservations made, and luggage carried from inn to inn, take note: some commercial tour groups offer custom-designed independent trips. Less costly than the full-up group tour, the independent trip still has many of the amenities, plus flexibility around your own travel schedule and complete privacy for dedicated family time.

*Credit card touring* is more of a do-it-yourself trip: you plan your own route, pack a few changes of clothes plus PJs and toothbrush into a set of panniers, stick your wallet and a map into your fanny pack, and take off. With cash or credit card, you pay others to cook your meals at restaurants and prepare your bed at night. Credit card bicycle touring is particularly convenient with a toddler or preschooler who otherwise might be a squirmy, fussy, or messy tentmate.

Planning your own trip is about half as costly as signing up for a commercial tour, even if you stay in the same inns. It involves, of course, more work, as you must map the route and make the overnight reservations; remember to verify whether the inn accepts children. You must also carry your own luggage and tools and be prepared to handle mishaps on your own—or plan a route having plenty of bike shops!

For any do-it-yourself multiday tour without a supporting sag wagon to pick up tired parents and kids, be conservative at first about your mileage estimates: 20 to 25 miles a day is about the right length at which to start.

## BICYCLE CAMPING

By kindergarten or first grade, many kids love the idea of camping outdoors. Bicycle camping, also known as independent loaded touring, is affordable even to families who are unable to consider a week of hotels.

### *What to Take*

For bicycle camping, each person will need to carry not only changes of clothes but also a sleeping bag, insulating pad (to cushion the chill and hardness of the ground), and eating utensils. Unless you can arrange to stay in a fully equipped lean-to or cabin every night, you'll also need communal supplies such as a tent, a tarpaulin (for a ground cloth under the tent), cooking equipment, and a stove plus its fuel (see Table 7-1).

Table 7-1

## MINIMUM EQUIPMENT NECESSARY FOR A FAMILY
## BICYCLE CAMPING TRIP OF ANY LENGTH

| *For the Family* | *For Each Person* |
|---|---|
| Saucepan with handle and lid | Plate |
| Skillet with handle | Cup/cereal bowl |
| Large pot with handle | Flatware |
| Collapsible water carrier | 1–2 Water bottles |
| Manual can opener | |
| Sharp paring knife | |
| Vegetable peeler | |
| Pancake turner | |
| Stirring spoon | |
| Slotted stirring spoon | |
| | |
| 1–2 portable stoves | |
| Fuel for stoves | |
| Portable barbecue grate | |
| | |
| Pack towel for washing dishes | Pack towel (for bathing and |
| Multiuse liquid soap | swimming) |
| | |
| Tent | Sleeping bag |
| Tarpaulin (for groundcloth) | Insulating pad |
| | |
| Paper towels | 2 padded bike shorts |
| Toilet paper | 3 bicycling jerseys |
| Sunscreen | 3 sets underwear |
| Toothpaste | 3 pairs socks |
| First-aid kit | 1 pair shoes |
| Tool kit | 1 long-sleeved jersey |
| | 1 poncho or rain jacket |
| | 1 helmet |
| | 1 long-sleeved camp shirt |
| | 1 dress skirt or slacks |
| | 1 nightshirt (oversized T-shirt) |
| | 1 pair water sandals (double as slippers) |
| | 1 swimsuit |
| | Toothbrush and toiletries |
| | Bicycle with front and rear racks |
| | Front and rear panniers |
| | Cable lock |

# Bicycling with Children

Standard camping equipment intended for recreational vehicle (RV) or car camping is far too heavy and bulky for carrying on a bike. You'll need compact, ultra-lightweight gear such as that used for backpacking, which is widely available in many camping goods stores and from mail-order catalogues. With such ultralight gear, a parent-child pair can have one two-person tent, one tarp, one stove plus fuel, two sleeping bags, two insulating pads, two towels, and two cooksets with utensils—all totaling under 15 pounds. Although the initial outlay for equipment can be a major investment, deep discounts are available from outlets; moreover, this is a one-time expense whose total price is likely to be far cheaper over the long haul than paying for a hotel room every night.

Although the number of items required for family bike camping seems like a lot to pack, they can be carried easily when every member of the family is big enough to ride a derailleur bicycle fitted with a rack and panniers (see Chapter 1, "Bicycles and Accessories for Parents and Teens"). Have every adult and child carry his or her own clothes, sleeping bag and insulating pad, towel, and eating utensils, while parents (and teens) share the weight of the additional, communal equipment—tent, tarp, stove, food, and fuel. Alternatively, load the extra gear into a cargo trailer that can be pulled by the strongest rider.

There are clever tricks for further reducing volume and weight. For example, use compression straps to cinch sleeping bags into the smallest possible space. Instead of hauling heavy, bulky terrycloth towels for drying bodies and dishes, use pack towels—small, thin rectangles of ultra-absorbent "miracle" fabric that dries quickly in air and sun—sold at camping outfitters. To dry damp pack towels, tie them to the top of your rack as you ride. Instead of carrying metal cooking and eating utensils, get ones made of Lexan, an extraordinarily durable, heat-resistant lightweight plastic whose knives even hold an edge. Even for a monthlong trip, each person needs only three days' worth of clothes—what is being worn plus two additional days' worth. (Actually, you can get away with two days' worth, but you'll be committed to washing clothes every night.)

Also, try to make most items function in at least two ways. For example, outdoor outfitters sell a multipurpose hot/cold-water biodegradable liquid soap that serves as shampoo and dish-washing detergent as well as soap for body and laundry—saving the weight and bulk of different bars and bottles. Instead of carrying pillows, each person can use a sleeping bag stuff sack filled with clean clothes. Consult any book on backpacking or a well-versed outdoor outfitter for dozens more weight-saving tips.

*Figure 7-4. Line panniers with white kitchen garbage bags to keep items dry in a drizzle.*

For ease in packing and locating your gear, develop the habit of always keeping the same items in the same compartment of the pannier on one particular side of the bike. Also, figure out tricks for efficient packing, such as turning a coffee mug upside down over the top of a water bottle. Remember also to keep the stove and its fuel in a separate pannier from the food and cookware and to keep snacks easily accessible in outer pockets.

For greatest confidence, work up to your first two-week bike camping vacation in stages. First, do day rides carrying all your equipment to get used to handling the weight. Next, camp out one night in the backyard with the new equipment, cooking dinner and breakfast outdoors with water from the garden hose, an experiment that will help you determine which items you should include—while you can quickly run into the house—or can discard. Last, try a local, overnight bike camping trip to give the family practice setting up and striking camp.

*Note:* Don't be deterred from the fun of sleeping in sleeping bags even if an older child is a bedwetter. Readily available in grocery stores and pharmacies are disposable, absorbent underpants for children 45 to 85 pounds, which are quite effective. For incontinent teens, try adult disposable undergarments.

*Tip:* Although panniers may be advertised as waterproof, do not necessarily believe the claims—a heavy downpour may seep through the seams and zippers. Line panniers with small or medium kitchen garbage bags—the 10- or 15-gallon white kind—twisted closed at the top; check the bags periodically and replace them when they develop holes (see fig. 7-4). Smaller zippered plastic bags can also make your packing highly efficient.

# Bicycling with Children

## Where to Go

Since bicycle camping frees you and your family from the necessity of finding a room every night, it also frees you to explore more remote parts of the country. Four scenic routes frequented by camping bicyclists, for example, are sections of the thousand-mile Pacific Coast Highway along the West Coast, the four-hundred-mile Natchez Trace in the middle of the nation, and the Shenandoah Valley and the Blue Ridge Parkway in the East.

If after completing a two-week bicycle-camping vacation the whole family is ready for more, you're already equipped to consider really big adventures! Bicycling across the entire United States, for example, has become relatively commonplace since the establishment in 1976 of the TransAmerica Bicycle Trail by the Adventure Cycling Association in Missoula, Montana (formerly known as Bikecentennial).

Since then, the Adventure Cycling Association has devised other east-west and north-south cross-country routes, as well as one from Montana to Alaska. It also has mapped a complete mountain bike tour along the Continental Divide. For each of these routes, the association sells complete kits of updated bicycle maps that show campgrounds, water stops, restaurants, bike shops, and other places of interest, complete with telephone numbers.

Need a bit of inspiration or convincing that such long trips are within the capability of minors? Check out four books recounting long-distance bicycle adventures with children. In *How Many Hills to Hillsboro?* journalist Fred Bauer recounts how he and his wife and their three children—ages thirteen, eleven, and three—pedaled from New York to New Mexico in eight weeks, starting out the spring before as complete novices. In *Hey Mom, Can I Ride My Bike Across America?* American history teacher John Seigel Boettner relates how he and his wife took five twelve-year-old students on a four-month bicycling field trip from Washington, D.C., to Los Angeles. *Happy Endings* by Margaret Logan is an unusually lyrical autobiographical narrative of a mother and seventeen-year-old daughter who bicycled the 2,000 miles from Paris to Rome in forty-five days, including crossing the Alps. And in the middle section of *Roll Around Heaven All Day*, Stan Purdum recounts a tandem trip with his fifteen-year-old daughter across Virginia, which included more than 30,000 feet of vertical climbing.

## GROUP RIDES—GOING AS PARTICIPANTS

If your family enjoys riding in the company of other cycling families, look in a local bike shop for any flyers announcing group fun or fund-raising rides.

## Group "Fun" Rides

Some municipalities occasionally plan a major one-day municipal bicycle "fun" ride just for the public relations value (see fig. 7-5). Such events may close down a city for part of a Saturday and have the atmosphere of a party on wheels. Some fun rides become well-known annual events attracting thousands of cyclists. For information about fun rides in your area, check local bike shops, community newspapers, the local chapter of American Youth Hostels, or such civic groups as the Kiwanis Club and the Elks.

Weeklong, cross-state bicycle rides are also sponsored by municipalities, bike clubs, community organizations, private vendors, and even state governments. Like municipal one-day rides, they attract thousands of riders ranging from infants to grandparents. Overnights are at campgrounds and high schools, spaghetti dinners are offered by community groups, luggage is carried by rented trucks, and the atmosphere is festive and relaxed.

Some cross-state recreational rides have become longstanding, nationally known annual events, such as the weeklong RAGBRAI (the [Des Moines] *Register* Annual Great Bicycle Ride Across Iowa, held every

*Figure 7-5. Group "fun" rides are enjoyable for whole families.*

July since 1973), BRAG (Bicycle Ride Across Georgia, since 1979), and GOBA (Great Ohio Bicycle Adventure, since 1989). Some have become so popular that bicycling families must register months in advance.

Cross-state rides are publicized the same way as municipal rides, and are also listed in the League of American Bicyclists' magazine, *Bicycle USA* and in the Adventure Cycling Association's magazine, *Adventure Cyclist*. Advertisements for cross-state rides also appear in major bicycling magazines and local and regional sports newspapers.

### Fund-Raising Bicycle Rides

If your family likes doing good deeds as well as having fun, look into one-day or weekend fund-raising bicycle rides. Keep an eye out for brochures in banks, retail stores, and other commercial establishments. Two organizations that have become particularly well known for their annual fund-raising bicycle rides around the nation are the American Diabetes Association for the Tour de Cure and the Multiple Sclerosis Society for the MS 75 and MS 150 rides. Call their local offices for information about any upcoming events in your state.

While some fund-raising rides are primarily for older teens and adults, others are set up to involve the whole family, including safe short courses for preschoolers. Participants often are treated to T-shirts, food, massages, live music, and other goodies donated to the cause. Be sure to inquire about the minimum level of fund-raising pledge expected: some are modest but others are quite high.

## GROUP RIDES—LEADING YOUR OWN

Since you've been having such a blast on family day and multiday rides, your kids are now begging you to plan a daylong or weekend group bicycle ride on one of their favorite routes for their buddies from school, their scout troop, or a religious youth group.

Hey, great idea. But how can you possibly keep track of ten to twenty kids? How many adult leaders need there be? What if some kids get hurt or have flat tires?

### "Point, Sweep, and Drop"

Since you'll be responsible for other people's kids, you might want to think about running a group ride the way a bicycle touring club or commercial tour group does. Not only does the structure they've evolved ease the task of keeping track of everyone, but it leads to a ride that is safe as well as fun.

Most clubs and bicycle touring organizations follow what is

known as the "point, sweep, and drop" system, named after the positions and different responsibilities of the tour leaders.

The "sweep" is the leader at the rear of the tour. The sweep should be the most experienced cyclist on the ride, ideally, a strong rider with at least a rudimentary knowledge of bicycle mechanics—that is, he or she knows how to change a flat tire—and a familiarity with the route. Why stick the most senior leader at the end? The sweep's responsibilities are to encourage tiring riders, to fix mechanical breakdowns, and to keep an eye on the line of riders stretching out ahead. On the open road, the sweep also warns the group of overtaking motor vehicles by calling out: "Car back!" or "Truck back!"—a call that the rest of the kids then enjoy echoing up to the front of the line.

The "point" is the leader at the head of the tour. The point's primary responsibilities are to guide the group along the planned route, to set a comfortable and enjoyable pace, and to judge when an impromptu "compression stop" is necessary to let everyone catch up for a brief rest. Firm rule for safety: no kids should be allowed to ride ahead of the point. In a group of preteens or teens, the kids themselves might want to trade off riding point. In this way, they gain some experience in reading a map or cue sheet—bicycle parlance for a list of mileages and directions—and keeping their prankster cohorts in check.

A "drop" is a leader for communication between the point and the sweep. No experience or knowledge is needed, although in some circumstances strong legs are a plus. In a large group or with younger kids, the drop may be any parent along for the ride; in a small group or with older children, the drop may be a child.

When is a drop nice to have? Sensing that the riders are tiring, for example, the point may decide to cut the ride short. He or she then designates a drop to stand at a corner to direct the line of kids to take the unplanned cutoff. The drop rejoins the ride as soon as the sweep rolls into view. In the event of mechanical trouble, the sweep might designate a strong kid to act as a drop, who then rides fast to the head of the line to ask the point to stop the group until the repair is complete.

On a ride with a large group—twenty to fifty kids—communication from sweep to point might be better effected by two-way equipment, such as walkie-talkies or cellular phones; for a smaller ride with an anticipated spread of under a quarter mile, you might also try inexpensive two-way FM radios.

## How Many Adults?

Plan to have one adult leader for every three to five grade-schoolers.

# Bicycling with Children

For younger children, you want an adult "segment sweep" behind every group of three to five kids, keeping an eye on the few youngsters immediately ahead. In traffic, the adult leaders can ride protectively to the left of the single file of children.

If changing traffic lights separate the large group into two or more smaller groups, there are still enough adults to act as point and sweep with each subgroup. If you need to cross four lanes of traffic, you have enough adults to act as crossing guards as the rest escort the children. Last, you want constant communication between the point and the sweep in case of an unexpected hazard, a child's tiring, or an accident. Unless you have two-way communication equipment, the only way to maintain constant communication is to have enough adults along the line so that each is within shouting distance of the next.

### Keep the Pace Slow

For grade-schoolers on 16- and 20-inch bicycles, 8 or 9 mph is plenty fast. Middle-schoolers are taller and stronger and are likely to have derailleur bicycles; they may do okay at 10 to 12 mph. On the ride itself, adjust the pace depending upon whether there are stragglers or whether the group is breathing down the point's rear wheel. As a rule of thumb, though, slower is better, especially at the beginning, because the kids need to pace themselves so as to have enough energy to complete the ride.

### Make Frequent "Compression Stops"

As a large tour group can stretch out for half a mile to a mile, plan occasional "compression" stops to allow the group to get back together again. Stop at prearranged places for water and juice—maybe where the kids can pick ripe blackberries or have an impromptu water bottle–squirting fight. Make sure to linger long enough at these stops so that even the stragglers have a good chance to rest before hitting the road again.

### If Possible, Have a Sag Wagon

A sag wagon is desirable, especially if the children are very young—ages five though nine—and the group is large—more than ten kids. A car is okay, but a van is better, as on a longer ride one or two of the youngsters might tire early and need a lift for themselves and their bikes. The sag wagon also carries the tools, the lunches in a cooler, a barrel of ice water for replenishing the water bottles, and a complete first-aid kit.

Also, make the sag driver the custodian of children's bike locks, keys, and combinations—you don't want a child to lose the slip of paper with its five-digit combination and therefore strand all the bikes linked by that cable lock. A car phone is also nice to have, if any of the riding leaders carry cellular phones.

In traffic, the sag wagon drives slowly behind the sweep with its flashers on to warn overtaking motor vehicles of something unusual ahead. If you wish, drape the rear of the van with a banner advertising your ride. At intersections, the sag wagon helps block traffic as a highly visible crossing guard. As a treat, the wagon waits at the terminus of bike paths and offers sweaty children cookies and cold juice.

### Take a First-Aid Kit

On a ride with ten to twenty youngsters, at least one fall is bound to occur—another reason for keeping the pace of a kids' ride at 8 to 12 mph. Most commonly, one child stops without warning and the child behind runs into the stopped bicycle's rear wheel, and tumbles to the ground.

The injury is usually a skinned knee, but don't pass it off—road rash really hurts. The segment sweep should shout ahead for the point to stop the group. Soothe the crying youngster, ascertaining if he or she is mostly scared or really hurt. Apply ice (if available) to the abrasion, irrigate it with cool, clean water from your water bottle, and spread on antibiotic salve and a small bandage. Check over the bicycle and helmet. Once all is okay, carry on with the ride. At the end of the ride, advise the waiting parents to clean the wound again with peroxide and apply more salve.

### Turn Bad Luck into an Adventure

If a thunderstorm sends you running for a barn or school, count the lightning flashes and admire the way the water turns the sides of the road into small creeks. If a child's bike gets a flat, use it as a chance to show everyone how to patch the inner tube—and let all the kids do a little something to help. Give them something exciting to talk about when they get back: "Hey, you'll never guess what happened on our bike trip!"

### Start with Three Safety Checks

Ask that the parents arrive with their children half an hour to a full hour before the ride is due to start, so that you can guide the group through a check of their equipment, the fit of their helmets, and a review of the rules of the road. Ask that the parents stay for these three safety checks; it may be the first time they have been exposed to this practice (see fig. 7-6). Hopefully your safety checks will help them set new habits with their kids at home. Also, this exercise should satisfy the parents about your ability to care for their children's safety.

Bring tools, including crescent and adjustable wrenches, and take a moment to show the kids and their folks how to tighten loose parts and apply motor oil to quiet squeaky chains and freewheels. Bring a floor pump with a pressure gauge, as—guaranteed—every tire will be underinflated.

Ask the parents to adjust the straps of the children's helmets so that they sit firmly on the kids' heads and cannot be knocked back off their foreheads.

Then gather all the kids together for a review of essential rules for riding in traffic and in a group, rules so basic even kindergartners will quickly catch on:

- Keep right and usually single file.
- Stop at stop signs.
- Signal turns.
- Point to and call out potholes, glass shards, and other road hazards to the person behind.
- Listen for the sweep's call of "Car back!" and repeat it for the riders ahead.
- Call out "Slowing!" or "Stopping!" when doing so unexpectedly.

Even if you are leading kids' bicycle rides several days in a row with many of the same children, *repeat the helmet and bicycle equipment checks and the review of traffic laws before each and every ride.* Repetition emphasizes the importance of these activities. You don't have to lecture them. Fire off crucial questions and make a game of who calls out the right answer first. That way they'll remember and will have psychologically bought into the rules.

### End with a Reward

Ice-cold watermelon is a huge hit at the end of a trip with kids, and helps along the celebration of accomplishment. It also offers a great opportunity for a seed-spitting contest. Homemade ice cream is also a reliable standby. Most important, congratulate each child on his or her achievement; for many youngsters, your ride may be their first-ever real daylong bicycle tour.

Tailwinds and dry roads!

Figure 7-6. Begin all group rides with a mandatory bicycle safety check.

# Chapter 8

# An Ounce of Prevention . . .

If you cycle a lot, misadventures are likely to happen. But don't let that probability discourage you. The worst effects of most common bicycling mishaps can be averted by forethought and preparation, whether your family ride be an afternoon spin or a summerlong bicycle touring vacation.

## SEEING AND BEING SEEN

Both for visibility during the day and in the event of being caught out at dusk or after dark, have all members of the family *wear light, bright colors*—bright yellow is the best. Solid colors are preferable to patterns, which to color-blind motorists have the effect of camouflage. For extra visibility, wear a bicyclist's international-orange vest with reflective trim.

A good psychological ploy is to fasten a bright international-orange warning flag to your rear rack so it projects a foot out to the left side of your bicycle. Motorists will give their normal clearance to the tip of the flag instead of to your body, buying you an extra foot or two of space on the road. A five-foot-high international-orange flag that waves over the left side of a trailercycle or trailer also increases your visibility (see fig. 8-1). For day rides, such flags can also make children on their smaller bicycles more visible to motorists.

To keep an eye on overtaking traffic without turning the head, *try using a rearview mirror*. For parents, mirrors that clip to eyeglasses or to helmets are most effective, because on a bumpy road handlebar-mounted mirrors often vibrate so much the image is hardly distinguishable. For children, however, handlebar-mounted mirrors are preferred, because they are less apt to be lost or broken. *Note:* As in driving a car, a rearview mirror does not eliminate the necessity of looking backward over the shoulder when shifting lanes or executing a left turn.

## PREVENTIVE RIDING TECHNIQUES

In motor vehicle traffic, never be in a hurry—even if you happen to be in a hurry. This calls for a kind of Zen suspension of your spirit if you're racing the setting sun. Being in a hurry increases the risk of not noticing a driver parked at the right curb opening the car door in your path, of not seeing a pothole or slick oil spot, or of not hearing or seeing an overtaking car as it pulls abruptly ahead of you to make a right turn.

*Figure 8-1. Attach warning flags to both parents' and children's bicycles or trailercycle (shown here) for extra visibility.*

*Ignore harassing motorists*—don't make the problem worse. Occasionally, teenagers in a car may harass cyclists with sudden shouts or thrown fast-food cups and other debris for sport alone; after their laugh, they pass on. Infrequently, motorists get absolutely livid when forced to share the road with cyclists; they shake their fists and holler out meaningless threats. Fortunately, these incidents are exceedingly rare, far rarer than super-courteous and cautious behavior from motorists. But you should be aware that at some point in your years of family bicycling, you may happen across a nut case.

Never throw down your bike and put up your dukes. The driver's car is bigger than your bike, and he or she is in the power seat. Instead, ignore them, and instruct your children to do the same. Ride on or pull over to the side, whichever feels safer in that situation. Smile and give a cheery wave, if you have the presence of mind. If they see they have aroused no aggression, even nut cases usually vent enough spleen by shouting, and will drive away.

Then report a description of the car and the driver, along with the license plate number, to the nearest police station.

*If a dog starts running after you, get off the bike and command:* "Go home!" Yes, your instinct is to pedal like hell, but few cyclists—especially younger children—are able to outrun a big dog. Moreover, you don't want to risk colliding with a dog at high speed, or having the dog run into you or, worse yet, your kids; some big dogs weigh upward of 100 pounds, which is double the weight of a first-grader. You also don't want to anger the dog by acting aggressively, such as trying to hit it with your frame pump, or spraying it with pepper spray—which may get into your kids' or your own eyes if the wind is strong or your aim is off.

Take advantage instead of the doggy psyche. Dogs are territorial, setting up a ruckus because you entered what they view as their turf.

At the first warning bark of a dog bounding toward you, shout "Go home!" in an authoritative tone. Get off the bike, put the bike between you and the dog, and walk along the road, continuing to command "Go home!" (see fig. 8-2). A familiar walking figure is one the dog is used to obeying, and normally the dog will prance alongside you, barking, until he comes to the edge of his territory. When you've walked past that, the dog will stand still and bark, allowing you to safely remount and ride off.

As scary as this sounds, it is the practice followed by organized tour groups, and it works.

*Cross railroad tracks at right angles.* If railroad tracks cross the

Figure 8-2. If chased by a dog, dismount, put the bicycle between you and the dog, and command "Go home!" while walking out of the dog's territory.

road at a diagonal, younger children should dismount and walk their bicycles across the tracks parallel to the edge of the road. Older kids may turn their front wheels perpendicular to the tracks and ride across them (see fig. 8-3). Be aware, however, that this technique may put them into the middle of the roadway, so they must stay alert for motor vehicle traffic.

## Keeping Tabs on Teens

Teenagers may want to ride ahead on their own, meeting only for snacks and lunch. If you feel your teens are responsible enough to head off for an unsupervised hour or two, set up several prearranged compression stops during the day when the whole family will gather together to do a head count. Lunch is an obvious time for a stop, but midmorning and midafternoon snacks or playground stops are good candidates as well.

Also, set a policy that if anyone gets separated from the family, everyone returns to the place where you were last together. While retracing all those miles may be an unattractive prospect, this policy can even undo a wrong turn. And make sure everyone has a complete map and cue sheet of the planned route. To cover all bets, you might even establish one phone number as a central message center for emergencies—or lend the independently riding teens two-way beepers or a cellular phone.

## CARRY ESSENTIALS

1. *Carry enough water.* On hot days, children may lose their appetites despite the energy they're putting out. Not eating is okay, but not drinking is dangerous. As is well known in the athletic world, thirst is a lagging indicator of the body's need: drink before you are thirsty.

   Make sure kids have enough to drink, and that they remember to drink it. Their little bodies dehydrate faster than those of adults. Stop every fifteen to thirty minutes or so to drink juice or water, and don't be surprised if each child downs two large water bottles every hour. If each bicycle is fitted with two water bottle cages, carrying all this fluid is simple. Refill at any available gas station or convenience store. Popsicles, frozen fruit pops, juice pops, Italian ices, snow cones, and watermelon are also excellent sources of fluids—and nice treats. Go easy on the ice cream, however, as it is not a good fluid replenisher.

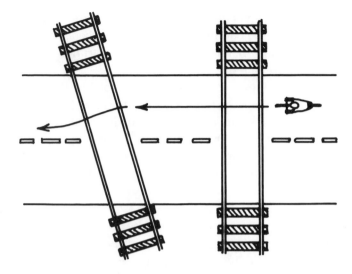

Figure 8-3. To cross diagonal railroad tracks, younger children should dismount and walk their bicycles across parallel to the edge of the road. Older kids may ride across the tracks at right angles, keeping alert for motor vehicle traffic.

Plain water is fine on days of average heat and humidity. But on hot days, bodies also lose salt and other electrolytes necessary for muscles and nerves to function properly and for bodies to avoid excessive fatigue. Sports drinks such as Gatorade replenish those electrolytes. You can also use rehydrating freezer pops intended for children with fevers; buy them in liquid form at a well-stocked pharmacy and freeze them at home (you can also freeze a sports drink). Fruit juice diluted by half is also acceptable in a pinch, although you really should also add a dash of salt. Avoid carbonated or caffeinated beverages, or ones with non-nutritive empty calories; really sweet drinks often make a person thirstier.

Despite all this fluid, your kids probably won't need extra bathroom stops, as they'll be sweating it all away. In fact, at the end of a really hot day, their skin may actually be coated by a thin crust of salt.

How can each person tell if he or she is drinking enough? Simple—if urine is copious and pale, all is well. But if little urine is excreted and it is dark yellow, increase the fluid intake.

2. *Carry a snack, no matter how short the ride.* As cyclists, you and your kids are the engines as well as the passengers. Even if you ate only an hour before, your body has a strange tendency to hit bottom unpredictably—and all at once.

Even for a one-hour after-school ride of 5 to 10 miles, a couple of snacks high in complex carbohydrates and low in fat, such as fruits and grains, will give adults and kids a quick energy boost. Good choices are granola bars, raisins, fig bars, and bananas.

For full-day or multiday tours, each rider also needs a stick of jerky or a packet of pretzels to replenish salt lost through sweating.

For an overnight independent bike-camping tour, carry one or two full emergency meals that can be reconstituted with water alone: good old dried macaroni and cheese, a can of tuna, several packets of instant oatmeal, powdered orange juice, instant coffee, raisins, and dried milk. If you arrive at camp late after the camp store has closed, you'll be thankful you brought this food along.

3. *Carry extra shirts for children to change into at lunchtime,* especially on a full-day or multiday tour. Even on cool days, kids' little bodies are sweating, making their shirts damp. After twenty minutes of sitting still to eat a snack, kids may become chilled and miserable. Riding after lunch creates a breeze that chills them even more until their shirts dry. And when a child is miserable, no one is having any fun.

Eliminate all that discomfort by tucking in an extra shirt for each child. The moment you stop for a rest, tell the child to change into it, and lay or hang the damp shirt on your bicycle in the sun. It'll be dry and ready for the next clothing change when you stop for the evening, especially important if you are camping out. Carry extra clothes as well for kids sitting still in a child seat or trailer; not only are children's small bodies more prone to hypothermia than adults, but child passengers are not exercising to generate additional body heat.

In some climates, a chill spreads over the land in late afternoon, even when it has been beastly hot at high noon. In other climates, the weather is highly variable and may include daily showers. Even if you're going for a summer day ride, carry an extra long-sleeved shirt or nylon or GoreTex windbreaker. Untreated nylon is not waterproof, but coated nylon is worse, as it won't breathe at all and will drench you with your own sweat even when you're sitting still. GoreTex is slightly heavier than nylon—and considerably more expensive—but it will keep you dry should you get caught in a light rain.

For spring and fall rides, also carry pullover sweaters for everyone. Choose wool, if you can, as it still insulates when damp with perspiration. Fleece is a good alternative—and is more widely available than wool in children's garments.

**4**. *Carry bungee cords and a few safety pins.* Bungees of various sizes are essential for lashing spontaneous yard-sale or fruitstand purchases onto the bike, or even holding parts of the bike together if you lose a screw en route. Safety pins can attach maps to your brake cables or hold together ripped clothing. The first time you use them, you'll know why you brought them.

**5**. *Carry a tool kit—and know how to use it.* At least take a spare tube, patch kit, and frame pump for repairing a flat tire. If you don't know how to repair a flat, another passing cyclist might be able to lend you a hand. (For some tips on basic bicycle mainte-nance, see Chapter 4, "Buying and Caring for Children's Bi-cycles.")

**6**. *Carry sunscreen.* Even on partly cloudy days, you and your children will be exposed to the sun for hours. Fair-skinned children, especially redheads, can begin to sunburn in as little as fifteen or twenty minutes, and can be severely sunburned within several hours. Ample medical evidence suggests that, even for children who tan, prolonged exposure to ultraviolet rays over a lifetime may lead to certain skin cancers.

Eliminate both the short-term and long-term risks of sun exposure by rubbing every child's exposed skin with a sunscreen rated at sun protection factor (SPF) 15 or higher. A number of products are designed for the sensitive skin of babies and children, with a variety of active ingredients. If one produces a rash, or doesn't seem too effective, try another—sunscreens perform differently depending upon body chemistry. Remember to apply the sunscreen under tank-top straps and the legs of shorts, as the child's movement will cause the fabric to shift and expose new skin. Reapply sunscreen after swimming or heavily perspiring.

Dress a child who is supersusceptible to sunburn in long sleeves of loose-fitting, lightweight, white or light-colored fabric. A soft visor under the helmet will shade the tender skin of the nose. You can also buy garments made of sun-shielding fabrics for both parents and kids.

**7**. *Carry maintenance medications and supplies.* If one morning you think you're going out only for a short exercise ride, the day might be so fine that you decide to stay out for a picnic. Keep your options open by being prepared.

If carrying a toddler, make sure you've packed extra diapers or pull-ups; pack one more than you think you'll actually need. Also take the evening dose of the antibiotic for last week's ear infection.

If you or a child requires some kind of maintenance medication—such as insulin for diabetes—take what you think you'll need for the whole day, especially if you've found that exercise causes swings in your blood sugar level. The longer the ride, the more important it is to remember these items.

**8**. *Carry a small first-aid kit.* While no one plans to be injured, children on bicycles fall more often than adults. It's nice to know you can clean and soothe road rash right when it happens. Many camping and sporting goods stores sell a light nylon pouch with sample sizes of bandages and first-aid cream. *Tip:* Triple antibiotic ointment is especially good, healing abrasions almost like magic. A few ibuprofen pain-killing pills of both adult and pediatric strength are also important to tuck in.

On a longer trip, you might want to add a chemical wrap that, when its internal seal is broken, becomes an instant ice pack. Such chemical cold packs are available from most well-stocked pharmacies in either reusable or disposable forms. The disposable type is lighter and more compact.

Similarly, guard against weather that turns unexpectedly chill, or provide welcome relief for aching muscles, by carrying a similar reusable or disposable pack that becomes an instant heat pack. Disposable heat packs are available not only at pharmacies, but also at well-stocked camping and sporting goods stores.

**9**. *Carry medical insurance cards and a handful of quarters—or a prepaid phone card.* This suggestion comes under the heading of talismanic objects to ward off evil. Medical insurance cards will come in handy if a youngster is injured or falls suddenly ill; the quarters are for making necessary phone calls. A lightweight cellular phone is even better than quarters, as you can call for help from a location far from a pay phone.

*Tip:* Have older kids and teens duct-tape a quarter or two to the bike frame where it can't be seen. That way they can always call home for a ride in the event of mechanical trouble, darkness, or injury. If you live in an area where bicycles are allowed on public transport, also include a couple of bus or subway tokens.

**10**. *Carry pencil and paper.* Not only are they handy for writing quick directions, drawing a sketch map, or jotting down the address and phone number of a newfound friend or delightful restaurant, but they also prove handy for gathering information in event of an emergency.

## MINIMIZE FLAT TIRES

Do you live in an area with an unusual number of potholes, shards of glass, thorns, cactus spines, glassy lava cinders, broken shells, or other sharp hazards? Do you and your bicycle—especially if you're toting the weight of your child—top out at more than 200 pounds? Does one of the family seem to average several flat tires a year?

The incidence of flat tires can be dramatically reduced by installing Kevlar-belted tires, expedition-weight tires, or extra-thick inner tubes. In addition, you can insert a plastic flat-prevention strip between the tire casing and the inner tube. *Hint:* Some cyclists report that the plastic flat-prevention strips themselves cause flats by rubbing the tube where the two ends meet; that problem is apparently solved by smoothing any sharp plastic edges with a file.

In most locales, one or more of these precautions are enough to reduce the occurrence of flats to once a year at most. If you and your kids are still averaging several flats a season apiece, however, consider more radical measures.

Certain liquid products can be squirted into an inner tube. The products are essentially antifreeze with fibers or little spheres that will plug punctures up to 3/16 inch. The products can be squirted only through Schrader valves—that is, standard automobile-tire valves—but then, Schrader valves are the ones most common on kids' and BMX bicycle tubes, mountain-bike tubes, and hybrid or cross bike tubes. You can also buy puncture-resistant tubes with the liquid product already inside.

Another solution is to install tires that never go flat—because they don't use air. One such product is Greentyre, which has a dry cushiony filling.

Be forewarned, though, that some cyclists find that both the liquid flat-prevention products and the nonpneumatic tires make the ride feel slushy, with noticeably greater rolling resistance than standard pneumatic tires. The liquid products also complicate the task of repairing a tire. Other cyclists, however, swear by the peace of mind of knowing the products protect them from being thrown by a front tire blowout on a high-speed downhill or from the urgency of having to make an immediate roadside repair—especially if the weather is threatening or darkness is approaching.

## DETER THEFT

A family of five with two adult bicycles, a trailer, a trailercycle, and a kid's bicycle, plus accessories, is riding on several thousand dollars' worth of equipment—even if some of it is entry-level or secondhand. At the least, the theft of just one bicycle by some lowlife will ruin the whole family ride that day.

Especially if you're riding in a metropolitan area or its outskirts, carry heavy-duty locks for the bicycles, and use them when the whole family sits inside a restaurant for lunch (see fig. 8-4). Make sure every bicycle has a lock passing through the frame and both wheels, and is secured to a sturdy object that itself cannot be cut or disassembled. Sit next to a window where you can watch the bicycles. Or have one older child or a parent stay with the bikes. Best yet, get takeout for a picnic lunch next to your gear.  Also, remember to register all your bicycling equipment with your local police department, the National Bike Registry, and the American Center for Bicycle Registration, so that your gear has some chance of being traced if stolen.

In rural areas or at a campground, such precautions may be less necessary. Still, you don't want the bicycles to blow over in the middle of the night, or be "bike-napped" by some skylarking kid. One or more heavy-duty six-foot cable locks can secure all the bicycles, trailercycles, or trailers together.

## IF YOU'RE CAUGHT IN THE RAIN

If you and your family get caught in the rain, ride extra slowly.  The biggest problem with rain is that it wets a bicycle's wheel rims, seriously reducing the braking power of hand brakes, and increasing stopping distance. This situation is especially hazardous with cheap toy-store

*Figure 8-4. Bicycles whose wheels and frame are securely locked to a sturdy object have less chance of "walking away."*

bicycles that have chromed rims, which get positively slippery when wet.

The only way to compensate for reduced braking is for you and your kids to slow wa-a-ay down.

Keep an eye open for hazards such as painted lines, puddles, and piles of leaves. The white lines that separate road surface from shoulder often get dangerously slick in the rain. Some traffic lines are not paint, but a type of reflective plastic that gets extraordinarily slippery when wet. Puddles can disguise potholes; at the least, the water may mix with engine oil on the pavement and make wheel rims even slicker. Piles of leaves may congregate over drainage grates; both leaves and metal grates are slippery when wet (see fig. 8-5). School your kids so that the first rider noting a hazard will point to it or call out an alert to the riders behind.

In a thunderstorm, you must also contend with strong winds. Such winds may be howlingly erratic, changing direction abruptly at

Figure 8-5. Piles of leaves may hide tire-eating drainage grates, and both leaves and metal grate may be slippery when wet.

corners, and threatening to blow you into the path of a motor vehicle. As summer cloudbursts may last only twenty minutes or so, sometimes the safest course of action is to pull under the nearest barn or awning—not a tree, as lightning is dangerous—and enjoy watching the fury until it passes.

## IF DARKNESS FALLS
Even if your family doesn't intend to ride in the dark, you can easily find yourselves doing so accidentally.

If night is overtaking you, hatch an alternate plan. Bicycling in the dark with young children is dangerous, especially if no one is equipped with adequate lights (aren't you glad you're all wearing light-colored, high-visibility clothing?). Changing plans is only inconvenient.

Designate one parent or teen to stay in a coffee shop with the younger kids while the other rides home fast to bring back the car. Or call a friend with a van to come get you and the crew.

If you're on a multiday trip with a tent and camping gear, you can set up camp almost anywhere—of course, you have extra water and your emergency meal, right? Or check into a roadside motel if one is available—wouldn't a hot shower feel good?

And next time when planning a family trip, build in enough time each day to allow slack for weather, mechanical trouble, or sightseeing delays.

### After-Dark Lighting Systems for Older Kids
Most kids on bikes assume that motorists can see as well as they can. They're wrong—and without proper precautions, they could be dead wrong.

Explain that by their forties, most adults no longer have the extraordinarily sensitive night vision of teens, and their pupils may be further contracted by prescription medications, such as that for glaucoma, or even plain old nicotine. Adult motorists may also be partially blinded by the glare of headlights from oncoming cars or by reflections off the windshield. Even if they do see the cyclist, they may misjudge the bicycle's speed, not realizing it could be clipping along at 15 mph. All these conditions are potential hazards.

Point out to your teen that according to the League of American Bicyclists' 1990 report *Lighting the Way Ahead*, the incidence of all types of traffic accidents triples after dark; moreover, forty percent of all automobile-bicycle accidents happen after dark, even though there are far fewer cyclists on the road at night than during the day. School your teen to drive the bicycle ultradefensively after dark.

In addition, make sure the teen's bicycle is adequately equipped for riding after dark. Although the Uniform Vehicle Code specifies a headlight whose white light can be seen from 500 feet to the front, that minimum requirement may be sufficient only in areas lit well enough by streetlights for the cyclist to see the road. Illuminating a dark road so the cyclist can see far enough ahead to ride at 10 to 15 mph is a much more stringent demand.

Halogen headlights are much brighter than conventional lights. Headlights powered by C or D primary (disposable) batteries, however, may have a discouragingly short battery life: even for an after-dark commute as short as 3 miles, the teen may have to buy new batteries as often as once a week. Lights powered by rechargeable batteries—especially high-end models in which the battery is carried in the water bottle cage—can emit a light as brilliant as an automobile headlamp, but may cost literally as much as a whole bicycle. Generator-driven lights, which are powered as long as the bicycle's wheels are turning, are cheap, reliable, and fairly bright, but at stops will abandon the teen in darkness.

If the teen cannot afford one of the high-end rechargeable systems, the most cost-effective compromise for adequate illumination is to *equip the bicycle with both a primary cell, battery-powered halogen headlight and a generator-driven headlight.* The battery-powered light will keep burning at stops and can function as a flashlight in the event of an emergency repair, both lights will illuminate the road for double brightness while riding, and the generator-powered light will burn as long as the teen is riding even if the batteries in the other light should fade en route.

The League's 1990 report highly recommends adding a red taillight. The report also recommends supplementing the taillight with red or amber flashers and red or amber reflectors. It leans in favor of amber, as amber flashers and reflectors are brighter than red ones. Amber is also more visible to motorists with red-green color blindness, estimated to afflict ten percent of men to at least some degree, to whom a red light may appear only as a dim gray or brown.

Taillights and flashers using ultrabright light-emitting diodes (LEDs) are inexpensive items at a bike shop. Many models are powered by one or two AA or AAA batteries, and have a surprisingly long lifetime. Many of the devices can be changed from flashing mode to steady mode with the flick of a switch or the push of a button. For a taillight, attach a red one set to steady mode to the back of the rear rack. Attach additional red or amber flashers to the rear of your left pannier or strap one to the left upper arm or left calf.

Remind the teen that, according to law, the headlight and tail-light must be turned on half an hour before sunset—possibly earlier than 4:00 P.M.—and left on for half an hour after sunrise—possibly later than 8:00 A.M. In part, this is to increase the bicycle's visibility to motorists driving directly into the setting or rising sun.

A teen bicycling after dark should also wear light-colored and, preferably, reflective clothing. Most cyclists' jackets have reflective trim across the yoke and the bottom hem. There are also high-tech fabrics that make an entire garment, helmet cover, or pannier highly reflective when illuminated by automobile headlights. Jackets and vests made of white, yellow, or high-visibility orange reflective fabrics allow a cyclist to be both visible in the daytime and reflective at night.

## IF A CHILD TIRES

"I'm tired! I wanna stop *now!*"

This is not too much of a problem if you're towing a child on a trailercycle, as you are still the primary engine.

But what if it's your eight-year-old on his or her own bicycle?

Even if dusk is approaching, take a deep breath—and take a breather.

Tired kids often recover quickly. Sit on the grass for a few min-utes and maybe tell a favorite story. When the child becomes restless and wants to run around and play, that is your signal for recovery: pro-ceed on your way at a slower pace.

Sometimes an expression of tiredness is a symptom of low blood sugar. At the rest stop, offer an energizing pick-me-up of juice, fresh fruit, and fig or granola bars.

Recognize also that an expression of tiredness may be an ex-pression of boredom, say, with a long hill. This is quite understandable—you yourself may be bored with the same hill. Counteract boredom by distraction. Sing fast-paced, blood-stirring marching songs. Play "I Spy" for objects on the side of the road—preferably ones up ahead that must be reached for closer examination. Set intermediate goals: "Hey, I bet I can reach that fire hydrant before you do!" For older kids, play an alpha-bet game, in which each family member competes to identify roadside objects beginning with each letter of the alphabet, in sequence: "I see asphalt!" "I see blackberries!" Last, bring out the secret weapon—an irresistible incentive, a.k.a. bribe: "You make it all the way home under your own steam, and I'll treat you to a double chocolate fudge cone for your accomplishment!"

If a child isn't moved by the anticipation of a favorite treat and seems listless after a rest and snack, perhaps the tiredness is the early onset of an unsuspected illness. In some people, the first symptom of a common cold is not a sore throat or cough, but an overall exhaustion, sometimes accompanied by fever. In this case, the day's bicycling is at an end. Send another adult for the car or call for a ride home.

## IF A CHILD IS INJURED

No one likes to contemplate the worst. But as parents, taking risks is part of the daily lump-in-the-throat job description of letting our kids grow up.

If a child falls—the most common type of injury—irrigate the road rash with clean water from your water bottle, spread on first-aid cream, and cover with a bandage (aren't you glad you have a first-aid kit?).

If a child catapults over the handlebar and ends up landing with the weight on one or both hands, injuring a wrist, try to keep the arm immobile while applying your instant cold pack. Get the child to a hospital emergency room, where only X rays can tell for sure whether the injury is a break or a sprain (aren't you glad your child was wearing gloves and a helmet?).

If the accident is partially or wholly someone else's fault—an unleashed dog bounding in front of the bicycle, a car cutting right in front to make a fast right turn—make sure to get all relevant license plate numbers, names, addresses, insurance numbers, and the names, addresses, and phone numbers of any eye witnesses (aren't you glad you brought pencil and paper?). Also, if you have a small portable camera, photograph the scene before the bicycle, child, and other party have moved. In the shock of the moment, you don't know what will be significant in an insurance claim.

### A Word About Sports Injuries

Children are more susceptible to athletic injuries than are adults because their younger bones, ligaments, muscles, and tendons are still growing. Moreover, kids may be reluctant to tell anyone when they are in great pain because they don't want to be left out of the activity.

According to Vincent K. McInerney, director of sports medicine and chief of orthopedic surgery at Saint Joseph's Hospital in Paterson, New Jersey, of particular concern are acute injuries (most often caused by a single sudden twist, fall, or collision) involving the growth plates, the areas of developing cartilage where bone growth occurs in children. Growth plates are often injured because they are weaker than the nearby ligaments and tendons. What may be only a bruise or a sprain in an adult may be a potentially serious growth plate injury in a young athlete.

Also of concern are overuse injuries, especially to the child's knees. The knees are the largest joints in the body, and absorb the greatest force loads. A series of small injuries can cause minor fractures, minimal muscle tears, or progressive bone deformities. Easing bicycling's potential stresses on the knees is one of the main reasons for teaching children proper use of low gears and making sure the saddle is high enough to allow proper leg extension.

The American Academy of Orthopaedic Surgeons, the Pediatric Orthopaedic Society of North America, the Canadian Orthopaedic Association, and the American Academy of Sports Medicine have a combined Play It Safe campaign, with safety and exercise guidelines that they recommend should be adopted by every young cyclist and parent.

In particular, they recommend that all children's sports—including bicycling—should be preceded by warm-up exercises and stretches that reduce the risk of a strain or a sprain (see fig. 8-6). They also recommend maintaining a healthful attitude by not insisting that a child continue to play or ride through the pain. Exercise-induced muscle soreness should disappear after two days; if it persists longer, the child needs to see a doctor.

## HEALTH OFF THE BICYCLES

If your family is combining bicycling with camping or hiking, stick to well-marked trails. Don't let your adventurous offspring go crashing off through the underbrush. In addition to poison ivy, poison oak, or nettles, off the trail children risk being bitten by a tiny deer tick infected with a bacterium that causes Lyme disease.

Lyme disease has been found in almost every state of the union (it is named after the town of Lyme, Connecticut). The first signs of the disease are often a large, red swelling around the bite and flu-like symptoms. If treated with antibiotics, recovery may be assured. But if unrecognized and left untreated, Lyme disease is a lifelong, debilitating illness.

Many county and state parks will provide you with informational leaflets on Lyme disease, rabies, and other health hazards. Read one and follow the recommendations, such as wearing long sleeves of light-colored fabric, tucking pants into socks, and examining clothes and skin when undressing for signs of ticks.

### Seat Straddle Lotus
Place soles of feet together and drop knees toward floor. Place forearms on inside of knees and push knees to the ground. Lean forward, bringing chin to feet. Hold for five seconds. Repeat three to six times.

### Seat Side Straddle
With legs spread, place both hands on same ankle. Bring chin to knee, keeping leg straight. Hold for five seconds. Repeat three to six times. Repeat on opposite leg.

### Seat Stretch
Sit with legs together, feet flexed, hands on ankles. Bring chin to knees. Hold for five seconds. Repeat three to six times.

### Lying Quad Stretch
Lie on back with one leg straight, the other leg with hip turned in and knee bent. Press knee to floor. Hold for five seconds. Repeat three to six times.

### Knees to Chest
Lie on back with knees bent. Grasp tops of knees and bring them out toward the armpits, rocking gently. Hold for five seconds. Repeat three to five times.

### Forward Lunges
Kneel on left leg, and place right leg forward at a right angle. Lunge forward, keeping the back straight. Hold for five seconds. Repeat three to six times. Repeat on opposite leg.

### Side Lunges
Stand with legs apart, and bend the left knee while leaning to the left. Keep the back and the right leg straight. Hold for five seconds. Repeat three to six times. Repeat on opposite legs.

### Cross-over
Stand with legs crossed. Keep feet close together and legs straight. Touch toes. Hold for five seconds. Repeat three to six times. Repeat with opposite leg.

### Standing Quad Stretch
While standing against a support, pull foot to buttocks. Hold for five seconds. Repeat three to six times.

*Figure 8-6. The American Academy of Orthopaedic Surgeons has developed stretching exercises for young people, which should be used before bicycling and other sports.*

## DON'T WORRY, BE HAPPY

Most important, maintain a sense of adventure at any opportunity—including mishaps—on the side of the road. Remember, if you know how to fix a flat, if you have packed rain jackets, or if you have some juice and fruit bars, minor mishaps are only inconveniences and delays, not disasters.

Kids take cues from their parents' responses to a situation, thus learning how to respond emotionally to mishaps themselves. If you feel like swearing or crying, don't. Instead, silently count five deep breaths, and then explain quietly what needs to be done. You're smart and you're prepared; you'll come up with a solution.

Also, have faith in your youngsters' resilience and ability to rise to the occasion. Children instinctively recognize when a situation is truly important. And they like to help. In fact, during a mishap they may prove to be buoyant and cooperative, even at an exceptionally young age.

Remember, to kids, a mishap—even a minor injury—is an adventure, the stuff of stories later remembered over hot chocolate. So enjoy your family rides, confident in the knowledge that you are prepared and do indeed know what to do.

# Appendix 1

# For Kids Only: Bicycling for Fun and Profit

Family bicycling—the focus of this book—is fun, but kids also want to carve out their own interests and circles of friends. Also, they may be able to earn pocket change or college tuition using their bicycles.

Here are some suggestions on how to help kids get started, beginning with activities that are accessible even to very young children. *Note:* Addresses for the organizations and magazines named below appear at the end of this appendix.

## BICYCLE RODEOS

A bicycle rodeo is a festive event that introduces a set of bicycle skills and games that can be tried and mastered by kids from preschoolers to high schoolers. While many local communities sponsor a one-time bicycle rodeo for a few hundred youngsters, some communities have turned them into enormous annual events attracting crowds of five thousand or more. Stop in at the various bike shops in your vicinity. With luck, you may find posters or flyers advertising local rodeos. Look also for ads or calendar listings in regional newspapers that cover bicycling and other sports.

## BICYCLE RALLIES

Younger kids—kindergartners through fourth graders—can go off on their bicycles together on the kids' rides at one of the major annual regional rallies sponsored by the century-old safety/advocacy organization, the League of American Bicyclists. There may also be separate teen rides.

Commonly held on the campus of a university where hundreds of families bunk in dorms or camp in the playing fields, the three- or four-day rallies include dozens of daily rides, lectures, exhibits, and the opportunity to test-ride various kinds of equipment, including tandems, child trailers, and recumbent bicycles. Registration forms for each upcoming rally—including the kids' rides—are published in the winter and spring issues of the League of American Bicyclist's color magazine, *Bicycle USA*.

## BICYCLE MOTOCROSS (BMX )

Inspired in the 1960s and 1970s by both cross-country dirt-bike motorcycling, called motocross, and the design of the small-wheeled, high-handlebar, banana-seat Schwinn Sting Ray bicycle, a new sport was born: BMX, for bicycle motocross.

The two broad categories of BMX are BMX racing and BMX freestyling—that is, bicycle acrobatics. Both have evolved into demanding youth sports with professional athletes competing for cash prizes. BMX has also revolutionized youth cycling, as virtually all children's bicycles—once modeled after one-speed cruisers—are now styled after BMX bicycles.

Despite the drama and the inevitable scrapes and bruises in organized BMX competitions, major injuries are rare. In part this is due to a carefully defined and strictly enforced safety program, including such equipment as motorcycle-style, full-head helmets, mouthguards, long pants and sleeves, elbow guards, and cushioning for the bicycle's frame.

BMX racing, which has categories for cyclists as young as age five, or kindergartners, is done on downhill, hummocky courses 800 to 1,400 feet long. In the United States, BMX racing is sanctioned by two major organizations. The American Bicycle Association (ABA) and the National Bicycle League (NBL), which together total more than 100,000 members, sanction races at some 750 tracks around the United States, the ABA primarily in the western states and the NBL primarily in the eastern states. Membership allows kids to tabulate and post points at any of their affiliated local tracks throughout the United States and Canada, as well as to compete in state or national events. Each publishes a feature magazine.

Although the ABA is the larger of the two groups, the NBL is affiliated with the Union Cycliste Internationale, which regulates international racing and world championship events. The NBL is also under the corporate umbrella of USA Cycling Inc. in Colorado Springs (see Road Racing and Mountain Biking, below), although it still retains its main office in Hilliard, Ohio.

The other kind of BMX competition, freestyling, consists of compulsory movements or tricks, as well as each competitor's own routines, as in gymnastics or ice skating. Competitors are judged by panels of experts, who look for both control and originality. Girls and boys can compete separately or against one another.

Freestyle stunt bicycles are single-speed, BMX-style bicycles that have a particularly strong frame, mag wheels—that is, ones with vanes instead of spokes—and handlebars that spin without being stopped by gear or brake cables. By standing on foot pegs extending from the front and rear hubs, riders can perform a variety of stunts on flat land, up curved ramps called quarterpipes, or even down ski jumps.

Younger readers might enjoy the pictorial introduction to both BMX racing and freestyling that appears in *BMX Bikes,* by Norman Barrett (New York: Franklin Watts, 1987). Older readers will enjoy *Bicycle Motocross Racing,* by Tom Moran (Lerner Publications Co., 1986). *BMX Bikes,* by Michael Jay (New York: Franklin Watts, 1985) also shows the basics of executing several freestyle tricks.

## ROAD RACING

Although there are virtually no organized nationwide programs for introducing youngsters to bicycle racing, there are effective informal ways for getting involved.

The best way is for a child to spend time at a local bike club or a pro bike shop where local racing cyclists tend to hang out. Some bike shops sponsor local amateur racing teams, and the mechanics, sales people, or manager may themselves be racing cyclists. Clubs and shops also are clearinghouses for information about local bicycle races as well as triathlons—races that combine swimming, bicycling, and running. Some clubs have a distinctly racing orientation, and offer regular training rides, coaching, and transportation to races. A good commonsense book that includes practical advice for junior racers, both male and female teens, is *Training for Cycling* by two-time Tour de France stage winner Davis Phinney and Olympic gold medalist Connie Carpenter (New York: Berkley Publishing Group, 1992).

A preteen or teen who excels in club racing may wish to become a licensed amateur racing cyclist. In the United States amateur racing all the way up to the Olympics is administered by the United States Cycling Federation (USCF), which issues racing licenses by age, sex, and skill; the youngest category is juniors, for riders under seventeen. Since 1995, the USCF has been under the corporate umbrella of USA Cycling Inc., which is the official cycling organization recognized by the U.S. Olympic Committee. USA Cycling's website has a wealth of information for boys and girls aged ten to sixteen who are interested in trying competitive cycling.

Encourage a would-be racer to analyze and learn from the techniques of top athletes, both professional and amateur. Watch televised annual long-distance bicycle races such as the Tour de France (raced in daily stages for three weeks each June), the ultramarathon Race Across America (RAAM), or the men's and women's bicycle racing events in the summer Olympics. Better yet, take the child to experience in person the thrill of watching a criterium (repeated short circuits around local streets), such as the annual Tour of Somerville in New Jersey or a track race at a velodrome.

## MOUNTAIN BIKING

Although riding off paved roads takes a youngster away from the hazard of motor vehicles, mountain biking does risk such hazards as falling on jagged rocks. Also, a child must learn to treat the landscape with respect so that vegetation is not torn up nor are animals or human hikers spooked by kids yelling and crashing through the underbrush.

Mountain-bike touring resembles backpacking on wheels. When combined with camping, it allows access to areas in the mountains and desert where roads don't go. An inviting introductory book for teens and adults with spectacular color photos and drawings is the *Mountain Bike Handbook* by Robert van der Plas (New York: Sterling Publishing Co., Inc., 1991). A heftier reference, which includes tips on off-road camping and buying a used mountain bike, is *Sloane's Complete Book of All-Terrain Bicycles* by Eugene A. Sloane (New York: Simon & Schuster, 1991).

Mountain-bike racing is fun for older kids who want terrain more expansive than a paved road or a BMX track. Races can range from friendly fat-tire festivals to intensely competitive individual or team events, including twenty-four-hour relays. Races are categorized into beginner, sport, and expert classes with girls and boys competing separately. Mountain bicycle races are overseen by the National Off-Road Bicycling Association (NORBA); like the NBL and the USCF, NORBA is under the corporate umbrella of USA Cycling Inc.

## SCOUT CYCLING MERIT BADGE

Is your kid into Scouting? Both the Cub Scouts and the Boy Scouts of America formally encourage and present awards for mastery of bicycling.

The Cub Scout awards are a belt loop, sports pin, and sports letter for participation by grade-schoolers. The descriptive booklet *Cub Scout Sports: Bicycling* (Boy Scouts of America, 1997) shows useful stretching exercises for children before and after cycling, as well as suggested rodeo routines.

For older kids, the Boy Scouts offer a cycling merit badge for the entire troop's mastery of basic mechanics, traffic-handling safety, physical fitness, and ability to map out and follow a bicycle tour route. The descriptive booklet *Boy Scouts of America Merit Badge Series: Cycling* (Boy Scouts of America, 1996) includes information about traffic safety and bicycle maintenance.

Both booklets are sold at well-equipped outdoor outfitters as well as through the Scouts. *Tip:* Make sure to buy the latest edition of the Scouting booklets, as earlier editions are so badly out-of-date about equipment and techniques that they actually advocate bad practice.

The Girl Scouts of America does not have a badge or patch specifically for bicycling. But it does encourage Brownie Girl Scouts to become proficient at bicycling as part of its "Try It!" program in sports and games. A Junior Girl Scout can choose cycling as the sport she wishes to master in working toward her Sports badge. And cycling is one of several activities in the "Rolling Along" Interest Project for Cadette and Senior Girl Scouts.

## BICYCLE POLO

Yup, it's a real game, first played in India about a century ago so that British troops could hone their equestrian polo skills. Now played competitively at an increasing number of middle schools and high schools as well as colleges, it allows active preteens or teens to enjoy some fast-moving, challenging, aerobic fun without the hefty price tag of a polo pony.

Because only one gear ratio is required, any kind of bike will do, including an old one-speed clunker. For a youngster already equipped with a bike and helmet, the only extra expense is about $50 for an official mallet and ball (which is similar to a miniature soccer ball—although a tennis ball, which is somewhat smaller, can be substituted); both can be ordered from the U.S. Bicycle Polo Association (USBPA). Elbow and knee pads are optional.

The object of the game is to hit the ball between goal posts at the opposing team's end of a field. Although an official USBPA field is a grassy area measuring 60 by 100 yards, a grassy level surface of almost any size will do. Soccer, football, lacrosse, field hockey, or football fields are ideal.

Each team has four male, female, or coed riders. A game or match is composed of four ten-minute chukkers, or quarters. Three major rules minimize collisions. First, all players must play right-handed. Second, a player may intentionally strike the ball with the mallet only when the frame of the rider's bicycle has been parallel to the sideline for at least three bike lengths—by which time that player has established his or her right-of-way. Third, intentional contact between opposing players or their bikes is illegal. In addition, the feet must remain on the pedals at all times, including when striking the ball; if a foot touches the ground, the player must ride out-of-bounds and then return to the action.

An introductory video, full set of rules, and equipment for bicycle polo can be obtained from the USBPA. The USBPA also offers discounts on equipment purchased by schools and some clubs. Mountain-bike polo is depicted, along with other mountain-bike games, in the book *Mountain Bikes,* by Dwain Abramowski (New York: Franklin Watts, 1990).

## YOUTH BICYCLE TOURS

Hostelling International—American Youth Hostels offers group bicycle tours exclusively for teenagers. Usually these events are student-budget affairs lasting from a weekend to several weeks, where overnights are spent in hostels or campgrounds and kids cook their own meals. They are supervised by qualified adult guides. Some multiday teen tours cover appreciable distances, such as from New York City to Montreal.

Older kids can learn tips on planning and packing for their own independent daylong or weekend road or mountain-bike routes and tours from the beautifully photographed book *Biking: An Outdoor Adventure Handbook,* by Hugh McManners (New York: DK Publishing, Inc., 1996).

## BICYCLE CLUBS

As there are some five hundred bicycle clubs in the United States, virtually every major metropolitan area—and a lot of smaller communities as well—has at least one. They range in size from a few dozen to upward of fifteen hundred members. Some clubs have a subsection specifically for its younger members or for the kids of its adult members.

Commonly, clubs offer day rides every weekend and perhaps during the week as well, starting from some well-known meeting place; rides are free to club members as well as guests and newcomers. A club may also have a relationship with a bike shop, perhaps using it as a meeting place. Shops may also carry various monthly club newsletters advertising their lists of rides. Bike clubs with full contact information are also listed by state in the annual Almanac issue of the League of American Bicyclists' magazine, *Bicycle USA*.

## BICYCLING ACTIVITIES FOR A RAINY DAY

Bad weather keeping kids indoors? Grab a book or rent a video about bicycling, or go to a bicycling museum.

There are bike books for all ages. The titles recommended below, which are listed aphabetically by title, had to meet a single safety criterion: cyclists must be shown wearing helmets—except in historically accurate nonfiction or fiction.

*Bicycle Book,* by Gail Gibbons (New York: Holiday House, 1995). Nonfiction. A general primer for younger children on bicycle anatomy and activities.

*Bicycle Man, The,* by Allen Say (Boston: Houghton Mifflin Co., 1982). Nonfiction based on an incident in the author's childhood in Japan around 1947. American soldier demonstrates stunts on an old cruiser bicycle at a Japanese elementary school.

*Bicycle Rider,* by Mary Scioscia (New York: HarperTrophy, 1993). Nonfiction. Children's biography of turn-of-the-century black champion racer Marshall Walter "Major" Taylor. Older teens might enjoy *Major Taylor: The Extraordinary Career of a Champion Bicycle Racer* by Andrew Ritchie (San Francisco: Bicycle Books, 1988).

*Big Bike Race, The,* by Lucy Jane Bledsoe (New York: Holiday House, 1995). Fiction. Secondhand bike for a first-class teen.

*How Is a Bicycle Made?* by Henry Horenstein (New York: Simon & Schuster, 1993). Nonfiction. Fascinating photographic tour of the Trek bicycle factory in Waterloo, Wisconsin.

*Olympic Dream,* by Matt Christopher (New York: Little, Brown, & Co., 1996). Fiction. Overweight teen gains health and self-respect through bicycle racing.

*Paperboy, The,* by Dav Pilkey (New York: Scholastic Inc., 1996). Fiction. A boy and his dog enjoy the predawn solitude of their job.

*Red Racer, The,* by Audrey Wood (New York: Simon & Schuster, 1996). Fiction. Bicycle envy.

*Supergrandpa,* by David M. Schwartz (New York: Lathrop, Lee & Shepard Books, 1991). A fictionalized account of a 1951 bicycle race in Sweden.

The movie *Breaking Away* (winner of a 1979 Academy Award for best screenplay, starring Dennis Christopher, Dennis Quaid, Daniel Stern, and Jackie Earle Haley) is a classic about the road-racing passion of a Purdue University teenager. Gives a realistic feel for the dedication and effort required. (The lack of helmets is historically accurate for the 1970s.)

Older teens with an interest in things historical—and the earnings to afford them—might enjoy the hobby of viewing or collecting and restoring old or antique bicycles. The United States has at least two bicycle history museums: the Bicycle Museum of America in New Bremen, Ohio, and the Burgwardt Bicycle Museum in Orchard Park, New York. Bicycles and equipment related to the history of bicycle racing may be examined at the U.S. Bicycling Hall of Fame in Somerville, New Jersey. Antique bicycles are also displayed in the Road Transportation Hall of the Smithsonian Institution's National Museum of American History in Washington, D.C.

Teens fascinated by antique bicycles may also wish to join the nationwide organization The Wheelmen, a national organization with its own library dedicated to the preservation and history of antique bicycles and bicycling. Among other events, they ride highwheelers and enjoy showing off costumes and fashions from the 1890s. See also the website of the National Bicycle History Archive of America (Santa Ana, California) at *members.aol.com/oldbicycle/index.html.*

Teens might also enjoy Pryor Dodge's full-color coffee-table book on historical bicycles, *The Bicycle* (New York: Flammarion, 1996). Dodge's renowned private historical collection is a traveling exhibition; for information on current and future venues, check his website at *users.aol.com/pryordodge/bicyclexpo.*

## EARNING MONEY WITH A BICYCLE

Not to be overlooked is the fact that a bicycle can help a youngster or teen earn money at an after-school job.

Although morning or evening newspaper home delivery is being taken over by adults in automobiles in some locales, in others it is still a good way for a youngster under driver's license age (eighteen in some states) to earn money—as well as learn the commitment, responsibility, and business management of a real job. Contact the office of your hometown newspaper for more information.

Enterprising youths have also set themselves up in a have-bike-will-deliver business by offering to deliver groceries, packages, or other items to neighbors and local shops. In many cities, bicycle messenger services are hired to deliver packages across town. Call local messenger agencies for information about training and jobs.

Kids who love taking bicycles apart and putting them together again can take bicycle mechanics courses and earn pocket change by repairing the flat tires of bikes belonging to friends and neighbors. Older teens may be able to apprentice themselves to a local bike shop to train further under professionals, or to get references to schools for professional bicycle mechanics (such as the Barnett Bicycle Institute or the United Bicycle Institute). Older teens or college students skilled in both bicycle mechanics and bicycle touring may secure summer jobs as assistant tour guides for commercial or nonprofit bicycle-touring companies—and have a lot more fun than flipping burgers!

Teens can learn safe riding techniques and bicycle mechanics through the Youth Bicycle Education Network, a loose organization of about forty bicycle education programs around the nation. Most of the programs aim to serve inner-city or at-risk youth who do not perform well in school or who live where recreational programs are in short supply. In many programs, youngsters who cannot afford a bicycle learn to overhaul donated bicycles, earning a refurbished bicycle of their own in the process. Several YBEN programs were outlined in the article "YBEN Uses Bikes to Motivate and Educate Urban Youths," by Craig Tower, *Bicycle USA* (January/February 1999), pp. 12–13. See also "When Kids Earn More Than a Bike," by Vicki L. Winters, *Bicycle USA* (September/October 1996), p. 25.

Even if a young person's after-school or weekend job has nothing to do with a bike, having an independent means of getting to work may make the difference between landing a job or not. In fact, bicycle commuting is itself a significant money-saver—if the teen or parent is disciplined enough to sock away the savings gained by not adding the teen driver to an automobile insurance policy or buying and maintaining an additional car. My book *The Essential Bicycle Commuter* (Camden, Maine: Ragged Mountain Press, 1998) focuses on Effective Cycling principles and addresses the particular bicycling concerns of young women, such as menstruation, clothing, helmet hair, and riding through questionable neighborhoods.

Last, a skilled BMX racer or freestyler might decide to turn professional, as have some of the stunt bicycling athletes winning medals in the X Games (the annual ten-day international alternative-sport Olympics held by Walt Disney Company since 1995 and covered by ESPN, ESPN2, and ABC's "Wide World of Sports"). Or become an entrepreneur with your own bike company, as did young X-Game stunt cyclists Matt Hoffman and Jay Miron.

Hey! You never know!

## ADDRESSES

American Bicycle Association
P.O. Box 718
Chandler, AZ 95244
(602) 961-1903
(602) 961-1842 (fax)
www.ababmx.com

Hostelling International—American Youth Hostels
National Administrative Office
733 15th St. NW, Suite 840
Washington, D.C. 20005
(202) 783-6161
(202) 783-6171 (fax)
hiayhserv@hiayh.org
www.hiayh.org

Barnett Bicycle Institute
2755 Ore Mill Dr., No. 14
Colorado Springs, CO 80904
(719) 632-5173
BBInstitute@juno.com
www.bbinstitute.com

The Bicycle Museum of America
7 West Monroe St. (St. Rte. 274)
New Bremen, OH 45869
(419) 629-9249
www.bicyclemuseum.com

The Burgwardt Bicycle Museum
3943 North Buffalo Road
Orchard Park, NY 14127-1841
(716) 662-3853
members.aol.com/bicyclemus/bike_museum/PedHist.htm

League of American Bicyclists
1612 K Street NW, Suite 401
Washington, D.C. 20006
(202) 822-1333
www.bikeleague.org

National Bicycle League
Main Office
3958 Brown Park Drive, Suite D
Hilliard, OH 43026
(614) 777-1625
(800) 886-BMX1
(614) 777-1680 (fax)
www.nbl.org

Smithsonian Institution Information
Smithsonian Institution, Rm 153
Washington, D.C. 20560-0010
(202) 357-2700
info@info.si.edu
www.si.edu/nmah

United Bicycle Institute
423 Williamson Way
Ashland, OR 97520
(541) 488-1121
(541) 488-3485 (fax)
www.bikeschool.com

U.S. Bicycling Hall of Fame
166 West Main St.
Somerville, NJ 08876
(908) 722-3620

U. S. Bicycle Polo Association, Inc.
P.O. Box 19424
Sacramento, CA 95819-0424
(916) 739-0724
(916) 452-7857 (fax)
usbikepolo@aol.com
www.bikepolo.com

USA Cycling Inc. *
One Olympic Plaza
Colorado Springs, CO 80909
(719) 578-4581
(719) 578-4628
(719) 578-4596 (fax)
www.usacycling.org
 * Umbrella organization for the U.S. Cycling Federation (USCF), the
National Off-Road Bicycle Association (NORBA), the U.S. Professional
Racing Organization (USPRO), and the National Bicycle League (NBL).

The Wheelmen
63 Stonebridge Rd.
Allen Park, NJ 07042-1631
www.thewheelmen.org

Youth Bicycle Education Network
(Vickie Winters and Harry Baker)
P.O. Box 8394
Santa Cruz, CA 95061-8394
(408) 457-2027
yben@cruzio.com
and
Charles Hammond
31 E. 52nd St.
Indianapolis, IN 46205
(317) 253-3632
chammond@iupui.edu
www.iupui.edu/ñchammond/yben.html

# Appendix 2

# Bicycling for Challenged Children

"My bike gave me the opportunity to be 'normal,'" recounts T. C. Hulsey of Napa, California, whose bout with polio as an infant left him without the use of most of the muscles in his right leg. He learned to ride a bicycle at age thirteen when he was able to convert from a full leg brace to a half leg brace. "Bicycling evened things up for me. My friends didn't notice I was handicapped any more—I was just another guy."

"When I was in second grade, all my friends got bikes and I found myself left out of things," says Cindy Wright Hammond of Ohio and Massachusetts, who was born without a left leg below the knee. But when she learned to ride with a prosthesis in 1963, "It was magic, totally awesome. Now I was able to ride with my friends to the grocery store, the candy store"—and by age eleven, in company with her cycling father and brother, she was covering 50 miles in five hours. "Cycling was an incredibly powerful and important thing in my life [from] ages nine through twelve."

"Often other cyclists I've been talking with for hours while riding don't even know there's a problem until I get off the bicycle," says Karen Mayberry of Kulpsville, Pennsylvania, who suffered a freak stroke at age seven that left the right side of her body paralyzed. "Do you have any idea how refreshing that is?"

In dozens of independent interviews with adults who have been physically challenged since childhood, the theme was unanimous. Bicycling not only gave them mobility and freedom—it was also the one thing that let them be normal (their word, not mine) instead of different from other kids, and at the one activity that is almost universal among children.

Bicycling can extend a challenged child's life expectancy. Many locomotor-disabled people do not die from their disability, but they do die prematurely—primarily from degenerative diseases associated with an inactive lifestyle, such as cardiovascular disease. As is well known, aerobic activities such as bicycling can help prevent such illnesses. As a low-impact load-bearing exercise, bicycling may not only fit well into a program of physical therapy, but also, because it is fun rather than boring, it may actually motivate a child to do needed exercise.

*Note:* The addresses for organizations and other sources cited below appear at the end of this appendix.

## USING STANDARD EQUIPMENT

Many kids with physical or mental challenges can learn to ride a standard bicycle independently with little if any adaptation of the equipment. Teens with learning disabilities, behavior disorders, or attention deficit disorder can enjoy independent loaded touring. (In the ten-day Bike Camp summer program of Camp Nuhop, a summer residential program for youngsters aged six to twelve, campers cover 35–60 miles a day on standard equipment.)

If sight, hearing, and sense of balance are intact, children with a leg brace, an artificial leg, or with only one arm can pedal an unadapted bike. According to Cindy Hammond, it is also possible to pedal one-legged without a prosthesis, but a prosthesis greatly simplifies mounting and dismounting at stop signs and red lights. Toe clips or clipless pedals—which are not standard equipment on bikes smaller than 24 inches—are essential for keeping the foot of the prosthesis from slipping off the pedal. Some locomotor-impaired individuals have gone on to become world-class racing cyclists, participating in the Special Olympics, where cycling has been an official sport since 1988. Events range from 500-meter time trials to 40-kilometer road races.

Neither are mild to moderate mental challenges necessarily a barrier to independent cycling, although the process of learning may require significant time and repetition. Since 1988, John P. Waterman, director of The Arc Cycling Program in Wayne, Michigan, has coached hundreds of children, teens, and adults with Down syndrome, autism, cerebral palsy, and other challenges not only to balance but also to negotiate their way on city streets through motor vehicle traffic—a skill that affords practical independent transportation for individuals whose disability disqualifies them for a driver's license.

Teens with severe scoliosis (curvature of the spine) or with shoulder or neck immobility can find independent freedom on a recumbent bicycle or tricycle. On a recumbent, the rider sits up with full back support in a chairlike seat and pedals with the legs extended out in front. Handlebars are either in front of the rider—above-seat steering—or below the seat where the arms naturally come to rest—under-seat steering, an option for teens with limited use of the arms. Recumbents are very comfortable, a fact which has made them increasingly popular as long-distance touring bikes; they have also been used to set many long-distance land speed records in cycling. Recumbent tricycles—popular among cycling commuters who live in slippery, gravelly, or snowy areas—may also be the answer for teens with difficulties in maintaining balance.

Because recumbents represent a comparatively small percentage of bicycles sold, their prices tend to be higher than those of upright bicycles, but several high-quality machines are now available for under $1,000. Alas, no commercial recumbents are yet manufactured in sizes small enough to fit younger kids. The only regular source of information in the United States on commercially available recumbents is *Recumbent Cyclist News*.

For children with visual or auditory handicaps, or conditions such as cerebral palsy that impair large motor functions, having them ride stoker on a standard or recumbent tandem bicycle is one way for the family to enjoy bicycling together. Richard Mayberry coaches sighted cyclists who wish to captain a tandem for visually impaired stokers (he can be contacted at the address listed at the end of this appendix).There are also a number of local and national organizations—such as the Pennsylvania Association of Blind Athletes—who sponsor training and rides, including multiday cross-state bicycle tours.

Recumbent tandem tricycles and quadricycles allow parents to enjoy cycling with severely or multiply-handicapped children. Recumbent tricycles designed for load-carrying have particularly strong frames and exceptionally low gears. Quadricycles—in which the four wheels are spaced like those of an automobile—are tandems that allow the two riders to sit side by side. The child or teen may pedal or not, depending on ability. Even a completely immobile child may enjoy the sensations of speed and breeze when propelled by an able-bodied parent in a bicycle-wheelchair tandem.

While these types of recumbent and tandem bicycles are comparatively exotic in the United States, they are more common in Europe, where most of them are manufactured and where cycling in general is more a part of daily transportation than it tends to be in the United States. A wide variety of European recumbent bicycles, tricycles, and quadricyles—complete with full contact information for the makers—can be found in *enCycleopedia: The International Buyers' Guide to Alternatives in Cycling* (York, England: Open Road Ltd., 1997). The buyer's guide (which is updated annually), informative videos, and other products are available in the United States from The Overlook Press.

## ADAPTED EQUIPMENT

In addition to standard bicycle equipment, alternative equipment specially adapted to different handicaps is available. Some adaptations may be quite simple—such as installing custom low gearing to give mechanical advantage to the limbs that are underpowered or large "training" wheels on a full-sized bicycle. Some special adaptations are pricey. But take heart: the outlay is often a one-time cost—and it may well make the difference between whether family bicycling is made a reality or remains a distant dream.

Older children and teens without the use of both legs but with full use of both arms can pedal independently with hand-powered bicycles available from Bilenky Cycle Works Ltd., Jesana Ltd., Special Purpose Vehicles, or Step 'n Go Cycles.

## ACCESSORIES AND SPECIAL GEAR

One aid that parents may find helpful for teaching balance to a child with physical challenges is a balance harness devised by Stephen C. Heinrichs of Dayton, Ohio, and available from Southpaw Enterprises. The harness can be used in the physical rehabilitation of both children and adults. Essentially, it is two strips of soft parachute nylon, each joined at the ends to form a circle; the two circles are sewn together at one point to form a figure 8. The parent holds the harness from the center of the figure 8; each circular strip is slipped under the child's arms, one crossing the chest and the other crossing the back. When the parent holds up the central seam of this lightweight harness, the child is securely supported. As the child learns to balance on a bicycle at slow speed, the parent gradually relaxes the secure support—yet the balance harness will prevent the child from falling if he or she leans too far to one side. With such support, the child can learn proprioceptic awareness—that is, the "feel"—of balancing. In addition, children from birth to age eight can try different types of adapted cycles, ride-ons, and accessories through the toy lending library program of the National Lekotek Center and its nationwide network.

With a bit of ingenuity, children and teens with challenges can be independent in camp as well as on the bike, assuming their share of tasks on multiday family bicycle tours. Look for standard outdoor equipment that simplifies the task of setting up camp, such as self-inflating insulating sleeping pads and tents that erect themselves when tossed into the air. Eating off paper plates with plastic flatware instead of using aluminum cooksets eases clean-up after meals. Striking camp is more complex but can be aided by equipment that folds itself as an umbrella does. Look also for telescoping crutches and canes that collapse small enough to be carried in a pannier or on the bicycle's rear rack. Such equipment need not be expensive or custom-made—in fact, lightweight folding travel canes can be found in well-equipped travel or luggage shops. Last, on multiday trips, carry petroleum jelly and moleskin to protect against chafing caused when appliances or prostheses rub against skin while pedaling.

For other suggestions about equipment and logistics, inspirational personal accounts, and ideas for international adventure-travel destinations, read *Able to Travel: True Stories by and for People with Disabilities,* edited by Alison Walsh (London: Rough Guides Ltd., 1994).

## ASSOCIATIONS

The U.S. Cycling Federation (under the corporate umbrella of USA Cycling, Inc.) serves as a resource for the disabled cycling community by identifying active organizations whose sole purpose is to serve athletes with disabilities (see contact information in Appendix 1). Also, Disabled Sports USA, a member of the U.S. Olympic Committee, oversees cycling events.

## LETTING GO

The biggest challenge is often not a disabled child's own capability to ride a bicycle, but the parents' willingness to let the child take risks. A parent's natural fear is that a child may be injured while bicycling, particularly when the child grows old enough to start pedaling in the street alongside motor vehicle traffic. That natural fear may be augmented in a parent who knows his or her child does not possess the reflexes, agility, and/or sensory-motor control that many other children take for granted.

But overprotectiveness is not the answer. In fact, overprotectiveness is what many children with challenges long to escape. "Parents think they're protecting their children by keeping them inside, but that's not true," objects M. J. Lowe, a math professor who had to learn to write and walk again (with braces) as a result of head trauma from a severe automobile accident. Now, with equipment adaptations, she bicycles 50 miles a day in the annual Bike Ride Across Georgia (BRAG). "What's the worst that could happen? They fall. But in bicycling, kids fall, grownups fall. They're not going to get seriously hurt if they wear a helmet and take precautions. Pick yourself up and do it all over again. At least if they fall, it'll be when they're doing something that makes them happy."

"If you fall, is that any different from any other kid learning to ride?" asks Cindy Hammond. "If I fell, my parents patched up my boo-boos and I went out to ride again."

"Limitations are more in the head than in the body," declares T. C. Hulsey, who as a teen took a tumble off his bike on a dirt course, breaking his polio-weakened leg in five places. "Normal kids fall, and normal kids break their legs, too. Kids all want to have fun—it's a universal thing. Just because you're handicapped doesn't mean you're an invalid."

## ADDRESSES

The Arc Cycling Program
John P. Waterman, Director
2257 S. Wayne Rd.
Westland, MI 48186
(313) 729-9100
(313) 729-9695 (fax)
thearcww@tir.com
www.comnet.org/arcww

Bilenky Cycle Works Ltd.
5319 N. Second Street
Philadelphia, PA 19120
(800) 213-6388
(215) 329-4744

Camp Nuhop
Jerry Dunlap, Director
404 Hillcrest Drive
Ashland, OH 44805-4152
(419) 289-2227 (phone/fax)
(419) 938-3221 (summer)
cnuhop@bright.net
www.campnuhop.org

Disabled Sports USA
451 Hungerford Dr., Suite 100
Rockville, MD 20850
(301) 217-0960
(301) 217-0968 (fax)
www.nas.com/dsusa/

Jesana Ltd.
979 Saw Mill River Road
Yonkers, NY 10710
(800) 443-4728
www.jesana.com

Mayberry, Richard
1351 Sumneytown Pike
Lansdale, PA 19446
(215) 855-6085

National Lekotek Center
2100 Ridge Ave.
Evanston, IL 60201-2796
(800) 366-PLAY
(847) 328-5514 (fax)
lekotek@interaccess.com
www.lekotek.org

*Recumbent Cyclist News*
P.O. Box 58755
Renton, WA 98058-1755
253-630-7200 (info line)
253-631-5728 (office phone/fax)
DrRecumbnt@aol.com
www.bikeroute.com/RCN

Southpaw Enterprises Inc.
P.O. Box 1047
Dayton, OH 45401-1047
(800) 228-1698
sheinrichs@aol.com
www.southpawenterprises.com

Special Olympics Inc.
1325 G St. NW, Suite 500
Washington, D.C. 20005
(202) 628-3630
(202) 824-0200 (fax)
www.specialolympics.org

Special Purpose Vehicles
Attn: Bill Darby
181 Elliot Street Unit 607
Beverley, MA 01915
(508) 927-3135

Step 'n Go Cycles
Attn: Stewart Lindsay
Treadle Power Inc.
Charlotte, VT 05445
www.stepngo.com

The Overlook Press
2568 Route 212
Woodstock, NY 12498
(914) 679-6838
(914) 679-8571 (fax)
www.bikeculture.com

# Appendix 3

# Recommended Resources for Parents and Kids

This bibliography is deliberately selective.

To minimize the necessity for annotations, I have included only those references that 1) show all adults and children wearing helmets, except in historical accounts where the lack of helmets is historically accurate, 2) conform to Effective Cycling principles as espoused by John Forester and the League of American Bicyclists, and 3) do not advocate techniques outside the Effective-Cycling purview that are unsafe for children.

Those basic safety standards eliminated a surprising number of references, including—frightening to say—some instructional videos from well-known safety organizations.

Any readers wishing to receive a comprehensive

annotated listing of references—including details about why the sinners omitted here are not recommended—may send a 9-by-12-inch self-addressed stamped envelope affixed with four ounces of first-class postage to Trudy E. Bell, 1260 Andrews Ave., Lakewood, OH 44107.

References below are grouped by subject according to the most relevant chapter in this book. I would greatly appreciate also being contacted about additional sources of equipment, information, and activities.

## CHAPTER 1. BICYCLES AND ACCESSORIES FOR PARENTS AND TEENS

### Magazines and Books

*Adventure Cyclist* (Adventure Cycling Association, Sales Department, P.O. Box 8308, Missoula, MT 59807-8308, (406) 721-1776; *www.adv-cycling.org*). Occasionally reviews racks, panniers, and tents as well as bicycles, and has occasional articles about multiday independent family tours.

*Bicycle USA* (League of American Bicyclists; see Appendix 1 for address). Keeps tabs on helmet laws and other state and federal legislation regarding bicycling.

*Bicycling* magazine (*Bicycling* magazine, 33 E. Minor St., Emmaus, PA 18098, (215) 967-5171; *www.bicyclingmagazine.com*). Sold on newsstands; reviews bicycles and accessories and also has occasional articles relevant to family bicycling.

*Cycling in Cyberspace* by Michelle L. Kienholz and Robert Pawlak (San Francisco: Bicycle Books, 1996). A guide to bicycling-related information through online services and the Internet.

*Training for Cycling* by Davis Phinney and Connie Carpenter (New York: Berkley Publishing Group, 1992). Detailed practical information about proper bicycle fit for parents as well as for growing preteens and teens large enough for adult bicycles.

### Mail-Order Houses for Quality Equipment

These mail-order houses also operate one or more retail outlets.

Bike Nashbar, 4111 Simon Rd., Youngstown, OH 44512-1343; 1-800-NASHBAR (24-hour number); *www.nashbar.com*

Performance Inc., P.O. Box 2741, Chapel Hill, NC 27514; 1-800-PBS-BIKE, 1-800-727-2453 (24-hour number), (919) 933-9113; *www.performancebike.com*

Campmor, P.O. Box 700, Saddle River, NJ 07458-0700; 1-800-CAMPMOR; info@campmor.com; *www.campmor.com*

EMS Direct, 327 Jaffrey Rd., Peterborough, NH 03458; 1-888-463-6367, (603) 924-7253 fax; *www.emsonline.com*

REI (Recreational Equipment, Inc.), Sumner, WA 98352; 1-800-426-4840, (253) 891-2500; *www.rei.com*

Sierra Trading Post, 5025 Campstool Rd., Cheyenne, WY 82007-1802; 1-800-713-4534

Bicycles, clothing, and accessories for women and adolescents under about 5'4" can be obtained from:

Terry Precision Cycling for Women, Inc.,1704 Wayneport Rd., Macedon, NY 14502, 1-800-289-8379, (315) 986-2103; *www.terry bicycles.com*

## CHAPTER 2. BRINGING ALONG BABY

For updated information on the status of helmet laws for minors in various states, contact the Bicycle Helmet Safety Institute, 4611 7th St. South, Arlington, VA 22204-1419; (703) 486-0100, (703) 486-0576 (fax); info@helmets.org. All this information is readily accessible on BHSI's website (*www.bhsi.org*).

*Bike!* by Amy Shepard (Grand Rapids, Mich.: Wee Venture Books, Inc., 1995). A board book that introduces preschoolers to basic bicycle anatomy.

*Big Bird's Big Bike* by Anna Ross (New York: Random House, 1993). A board book for preschoolers in which the popular Sesame Street character comes to understand the importance of brakes.

## CHAPTER 3. TANDEM CYCLING: PARENT-CHILD TEAMWORK

### Books and Magazines

*The Tandem Scoop: An Insider's Guide to Tandem Cycling* by John Schubert (Eugene, Ore.: Burley Design Cooperative, 1993). The only all-around introduction to tandem bicycling—including chapters on tandeming with families and with disabled stokers.

*Tandem & Family Cycling Magazine*, P.O. Box 2939, Eugene, OR 97402; (541) 485-5262, (541) 302-1950 (fax); subscriptions@tandemmag.com; *www.tandemmag.com*. A quarterly that reviews trailercycles, tandem bicycles, and tandem-riding events. It also features classified ads offering used equipment.

## Equipment

ATB Greengear of Eugene, Oregon, has introduced a tandem bicycle specifically designed for parents and kids. Called the Family Tandem, it features 21-speed gearing and instantly adjustable sizing both for the captain's and stoker's positions. As the one bike can accommodate captains ranging from 5' to 6'5", both Mom and Dad could switch off riding with the stokid—or the parents can ride together. With the small-child kit, the stoker's position can accommodate a child ranging from 36" to 55" tall; with the large-child/adult kit, the stoker's position can accommodate a stoker from 54" to 6'2". The bicycle, which has 20-inch wheels, folds for shipping, storing, or wedging into a car.

For information about the Family Tandem, contact ATB Greengear, 4065 W. 11th Ave. #14, Eugene, OR 97402; 1-800-777-0258, (541) 687-0487, (541) 687-0403 (fax); *www.greengear.com*

At least one manufacturer has also introduced a tandem sized just for kids: Longbikes, 8160 Blakeland Dr., Unit D, Littleton, CO 80125; 1-877-TANDEMS or (303) 471-6700, (303) 471-6705 (fax); *www.tandem bike.com*

As of this writing, there is no general reference other than this book on trailercycles. For information about the principal designs, contact a local bicycle shop or write directly to the manufacturers below for information:

Adams Trail-A-Bike
Norco Products Ltd.
1465 Kebet Way
Port Coquitlam, B.C. V3C 6L37
Canada
(604) 552-2930
(604) 552-2931 (fax)
www.grofa.com/grofa/adams.htm

Bike-A-Long Inc.
111 boul. de l'Hôpital, Suite 202
Gatineau, Quebec J87 7V1
Canada
(888) 799-BIKE (2453)
(888) 799-2009 (fax)
www.bikealong.com

Burley Piccolo trailercycle and child trailers
Burley Design Cooperative
4020 Stewart Rd.
Eugene, OR 97402
(800) 311-5294
(541) 687-1644
(541) 687-0436 (fax)
www.burley.com

## CHAPTER 4. BUYING AND CARING FOR CHILDREN'S BICYCLES

As of this writing, there is no general reference other than this book on how to buy a children's bicycle. There are a number of titles, however, that cover secondhand bikes and repair.

"Rehabilitating a Second-Hand Bicycle" in *The Essential Bicycle Commuter* by Trudy E. Bell (Camden, Maine: Ragged Mountain Press, 1998). Provides detailed information on how to buy and restore a secondhand bicycle.

Chapter 36, "Commuting and Utility Cycling," in *Effective Cycling* by John Forester (Cambridge, Mass.: MIT Press, 1993). Instructions for building a "trashmobile" from found parts.

*Richards' Ultimate Bicycle Book* by Richard Ballantine and Richard Grant (New York: Dorling Kindersley, 1992). Large-format book with superb photography.

*Bicycling Magazine's Complete Guide to Bicycle Maintenance and Repair* (Emmaus, Penn.: Rodale Press, 1994). A classic.

*Glenn's New Complete Bicycle Manual* by Clarence W. Coles, Harold T. Glenn, and John S. Allen (New York: Crown Publishers Inc., 1987). The revision of a work published in 1973 at the height of the bike boom, it contains much relevant information on repairing and maintaining older bicycles that you might obtain secondhand.

## CHAPTER 5. LEARNING TO RIDE

Little has been written on ways of teaching children to balance and ride a bicycle. And while many books on bicycling have chapters devoted to the effective use of derailleur gears and techniques for downshifting on hills, none is geared (pun intended) specifically toward children.

"Teaching Your Child to Ride." One of a series of instructional leaflets published by *Bicycling* magazine, available for free at some bike shops.

*Pedal Magic* (17 minutes, 1996). This instructional video details Reginald Joules's effective technique for teaching a child to balance plus extra exercises for unlearning bad habits from training wheels. (Available from Reginald's Pedal Magic Inc., c/o Cherokee Productions, P.O. Box 2995, Littleton, CO 80161-2995; Reginald Joules may be reached directly at (303) 850-0947 or via e-mail at rjoules@earthlink.net).

Some fictional stories may encourage children who are trying to learn to balance by showing that they are not alone in their frustration.

*D.W. Rides Again!* by Marc Brown (New York: Little, Brown & Co., 1993). This book may encourage children who are learning to balance. Arthur's spunky younger sister learns how to ride without training wheels (the video by the same title is more complete in showing the sister's persistence through frustration).

*Franklin Rides a Bike,* by Paulette Bourgeois and Brenda Clark (New York: Scholastic Inc., 1997). A young turtle finds it hard to ride a bike without training wheels.

*I Would If I Could,* by Betty Miles (New York: Alfred A. Knopf, Inc., 1982). In this story set in 1938, a girl is afraid that she is the only ten-year-old in the world who doesn't know how to ride a bicycle—and persists all summer until she does. The lack of helmets is historically accurate for the 1930s.

*Magic Bicycle, The,* by Berlie Doherty (New York: Crown Publishers, Inc., 1995). Illustrates the persistence needed for a young boy to learn to ride a bicycle—and also the scary ineffectiveness of the "Dad" learning technique. Eventually visualization and persistence win the day. Beautifully painted illustrations.

*Mrs. Peachtree's Bicycle,* by Erica Silverman (New York: Simon & Schuster, 1996). Story of an older woman who persists in learning to ride a bicycle for practical transportation during the bicycle craze at the turn of the century, despite the fact that "wheeling" was regarded as unseemly for women. The lack of helmets is historically accurate for the 1890s.

*My Bike,* by Donna Jakob (New York: Hyperion Books for Children, 1994). A boy describes the difference between yesterday (when he was struggling to ride a bike) and today (when he leads all bicyclists).

## CHAPTER 6. TEACHING TRAFFIC SAFETY TO CHILDREN

### Printed Materials for Teens and Parents

*Effective Cycling* by John Forester (Cambridge, Mass.: MIT Press, 1993). This classic book is the fundamental text for the Effective Cycling instruction program offered by the League of American Bicyclists and the federal government's Uniform Vehicle Code (for courses, see below).

"Bicycle Safety: What Every Parent Should Know," by John E. Williams (available from the Adventure Cycling Association; see Appendix 1 for address and phone). An excellent leaflet showing the principal types of traffic mistakes children make, and what to teach children. Although published in 1981, much of its advice is still timely.

*The Guide to Bicycle Rodeos* by John Williams and Dan Burden (available from the Adventure Cycling Association; see Appendix 1 for address and phone). This booklet contains more than a dozen skills tests set up as games, which teach kids important reflexes for bicycling in the street with motor vehicle traffic.

Bicycle Rodeo Kit (workbooks, brochures, mechanical checklists, certificates of achievement, bicycle driver's licenses, braking reaction test rulers, and skills stations posters). Kit provides materials necessary for staging a bicycle rodeo for up to 100 participants (available from Publications Department, Outdoor Empire Publishing, Inc., 511 Eastlake Avenue East, Seattle, WA 98109; (206) 624-3845).

### Books for Children

*Safety on Bicycles* by K. Carter (Vero Beach, Florida: The Rourke Press, Inc., 1994). A simple and general introduction to bicycling safety that can be read even to kindergartners.

### Bicycling Instructional Videos

*A Kids' Eye View* (10+ minutes, 1994). An illuminating look (for teens and parents) at a group bicycle ride with half a dozen gradeschoolers, showing changes before and after safety instruction. (Produced by the Office of Transportation Safety, Wisconsin Dept. of Transportation, and available from the League of American Bicyclists; see Appendix 1 for address and phone.)

*Bicycle Safety Camp* (25 minutes, 1989). Produced in cooperation with The Injury Prevention Program of the American Academy of Pediatrics, this video is particularly appropriate for ages five through nine. (Available from David Lewine & Associates, Inc., 914 Montana Ave., Santa Monica, CA 90069; (310) 657-5782.)

*Bicycle Safety First* (13 minutes, 1992). For ages twelve through adult, especially teens and parents graduating to bicycle commuting, long-distance day rides, or multiday tours. (Available from Tim Kneeland & Associates, 200 Lake Washington Blvd., Suite 101, Seattle, WA 98122-6540; (206) 322-4102, (800) 433-0528.)

*Biking: Get the Big Picture* (8 minutes, 1994). Most of the information is correct, although the child's helmet is loose and he says he is riding a bike only until he is old enough to drive a car. For sixth- to eighth- graders. (Available from AAA Foundation for Traffic Safety, 1440 New York Ave. NW, Washington, D.C. 20005; (202) 638-5944, (800) 305-SAFE; also, P.O. Box 8257, Fredericksburg, VA 22404; (540) 372-4405 (fax); *www.aaafts.org/aaa/*.)

*Effective Cycling Video* (41 minutes, 1994). Based on John Forester's book. Probably the most complete instructional video in existence on bicycling traffic safety. For older kids, teens, and parents. (Available from Seidler Productions, 191 Pine Lane, Crawfordville, FL 32327-9452; (904) 925-6331.)

## Bicycling Courses

The League of American Bicycling offers three family-bicycling courses: Kids I (for parents of children aged four to nine), Kids II (for youths aged ten to twelve), and Kids III (for youths aged thirteen to fifteen), all of which are based on John Forester's Effective Cycling principles (for the address of the League, see Appendix 1).

## CHAPTER 7. FAMILY AND GROUP RIDES

### Guides for Road Tours

*Family Bicycling in the Washington-Baltimore Area* by John Pescatore (McLean, Virginia: EPM Publications Inc., 1993). The only regional guide with twenty-eight kid-tested off-the-beaten-path route maps.

*Bicycling Around New York City: A Gentle Touring Guide* by Trudy E. Bell (Birmingham, Ala.: Menasha Ridge Press,1994). Features easy rides from 8 to 45 miles long in upstate New York, New Jersey, Connecticut, and Long Island. Although written for novice adult cyclists, it has many suggestions for riding with kids, and some rides are primarily on paved bike paths, canal towpaths, or aqueduct trails.

## Bicycling with Children

*Short Bike Rides* . . . . (Old Saybrook, Conn.: The Globe Pequot Press, various). This series of regional guides has many rides adaptable to families and children.

### Guides to Canal Towpaths and Rail Trails

The best source of detailed maps and mile-by-mile booklet or book-length guides to individual canal towpaths are various local canal historical societies. For more information, contact the American Canal Society, P.O. Box 842, Shepherdstown, WV 25443; *www.blacksheep.org /canals/ACS/acs.html.*

*700 Great Rail-Trails* by Greg Smith and Karen-Lee Ryan (Washington, D.C.: Rails-to-Trails Conservancy, 1995). A simple listing of all the rail trails in the United States. The Conservancy has also published several books with full descriptions and detailed maps of all the rail trails in individual states, including Michigan, Illinois, Indiana, Pennsylvania, and the Mid-Atlantic states (for a complete listing, contact the Rails-to-Trails Conservancy, 1100 17th Street NW, 10th Floor, Washington, D.C. 20036; (202) 331-9696; *www.railtrails.org*).

*Biking Ohio's Rail-Trails: Where to Go, What to Expect, How to Get There* by Shawn E. Richardson (Cambridge, Minn.: Adventure Publications, 1996). Includes detailed maps on the 20-mile-long towpath trail between Cleveland and Akron along the Ohio & Erie Canal.

*Washington's Rail-Trails: A Guide for Walkers, Bicyclists, Equestrians* by Fred Wert (Seattle: The Mountaineers, 1992). Includes descriptions of some twenty trails suitable for bicycling.

### Maps

The DeLorme Mapping Company has published individual *Atlas & Gazetteers* for about half the states. Widely available in book and map stores, these large-format books of topographic maps show both paved and dirt roads as well as suggested bicycle routes; they also list wildlife areas and other local attractions. (DeLorme Mapping Co., P.O. Box 298, Freeport, ME 04032; (800) 227-1656)

County maps for all fifty states can be ordered from County Maps, 821 Puetz Place, Lyndon Station, WI 53844; (608) 666-3331.

### Group Bicycle Tours

Cross-state, cross-country, and shorter bicycle tours in the United States and overseas offered by various organizations—including ones that accept children—are listed in both the Adventure Cycling Association's annual *The Cyclists' Yellow Pages* and the annual "Tourfinder" issue of *Bicycle USA* (the magazine of the League of American Bicyclists).

An up-to-date list of multiday group fun rides in North America with contact information is also maintained on the website of the National Bicycle Tour Directors Association at *www.okfreewheel.com/nbtda .html*.

At least two commercial tour operators offer bicycle vacations specifically for families, even ones with very young children. The two-decade-old California-based company Backroads offers both camping and inn family tours (Backroads, 801 Cedar St., Berkeley, CA 94710-1800; 1-800-462-2848; goactive@backroads.com; *www.backroads.com*). The Canadian company Freewheeling Adventures offers inn tours (Freewheeling Adventures Inc., RR#1, The Lodge, Hubbards, NS, Canada, B0J 1T0; 902-857-3600, 902-857-3612 (fax); bicycle@freewheeling.ca; *www.freewheeling.ca*).

## Multiday Independent Family Touring

*The Bicycle Touring Manual: Using the Bicycle for Touring and Camping* by Rob van der Plas (Mill Valley, Calif.: Bicycle Books Inc., 1993). Includes chapters on touring with children, tandem touring, mountain bike touring, planning a tour, and touring in any kind of weather (unfortunately, van der Plas is casual about helmets).

*The Essential Touring Cyclist: A Complete Course for the Bicycle Traveler* by Richard A. Lovett (Camden, Maine: Ragged Mountain Press, 1994). Includes chapters on credit-card touring, organized tours, and dealing with aches and pains (scrapes, bug bites, and the like).

*Bike Touring: The Sierra Club Guide to Outings on Wheels* by Raymond Bridge (Sierra Club Books, 1979). Although out of print, this book and the following title can often be found in secondhand book stores and are highly recommended for families or teens who want to try independent bicycle touring.

*Freewheeling: the Bicycle Camping Book* by Raymond Bridge (Harrisburg, Penn.: Stackpole Books, 1974).

*Are We Having Fun Yet? Enjoying the Outdoors with Partners, Families, and Groups* by Brian Baird (Seattle: The Mountaineers, 1995). An insightful book on the psychology of parents and kids enjoying a happy outdoor adventure together—including communicating over differences in expectations.

*Adventuring with Children: The Complete Manual for Family Adventure Travel* by Nan Jeffrey, 2nd ed. (Santa Rosa, Calif.: Foghorn Press, 1992). Includes chapters on bicycling, camping, traveling with infants, and international destinations.

*Fodor's Family Adventures: More Than 500 Great Trips for You and Your Kids of All Ages* (New York: Fodor's Travel Publications, Inc., 1996). One chapter on bicycling, including a descriptive listing of outfitters offering commercial bicycle tours for parents and kids in the United States.

*Outdoor Adventures with Kids,* by Mary Mapes McConnell (Dallas: Taylor Publishing Co., 1996). Good general advice on strengthening family bonds on the trail. Nothing specifically about bicycling, but much helpful advice about off-the-bike activities (backpacking, canoeing, rafting, kayaking) that you might want to combine with cycling on an independent bicycle vacation.

## Leading Groups of Children

There are no books published on how to lead group tours of either children or adults, although the American Youth Hostels has a formal program to train bicycle tour leaders.

"'Thrilled to Be Adventuring: Leading Group Rides for Children," by Trudy E. Bell, in *Bicycle USA* (the magazine of the League of American Bicyclists) (September/October 1996), p. 53.

## Accounts of Long-Distance Family Bicycle Tours

*How Many Hills to Hillsboro?* by Fred Bauer (Tappan, New Jersey: Hewitt House, 1969). (Photos show family without helmets—but then, this was 1968).

*Hey, Mom, Can I Ride My Bike Across America?* by John Seigel Boettner (Brea, Calif.: Seigel Boettner Fulton, 1990).

*Happy Endings,* by Margaret Logan (Boston: Houghton Mifflin Co., 1979).

*Roll Around Heaven All Day: A Piecemeal Journey Across America by Bicycle,* by Stan Purdum (Canton, Ohio: Communication Resources Inc., 1997).

*Bike Trip,* by Betsy and Giulio Maestro (New York: HarperCollins, 1992). A fictional picture book for younger children that conveys the exhilaration of a young boy's independently riding 16 miles with his parents and sister on his first daylong bicycle tour. Accurately portrays good safety practice, the physical sensations, the hard work, the fun, and the triumph.

## CHAPTER 8. AN OUNCE OF PREVENTION . . .

As of this writing, little besides this book has been written specifically about handling non-repair roadside emergencies involving bicycling children or families.

*Lighting the Road Ahead,* (League of American Bicyclists, 1990). A report on bicycle lighting and night riding with useful analysis of varying statewide requirements and suggestions for maximum safety.

"Play It Safe." A brochure showing warm-up stretching exercises recommended for athletic children. (For a free copy, send a stamped self-addressed envelope to Play It Safe, American Academy of Orthopaedic Surgeons, P.O. Box 1998, Des Plaines, IL 60018; (800) 824-BONE.)

Clothing of special sun-protection fabrics (SPF 30+) for both children and adults can be ordered from:

Sun Precautions, 2815 Wetmore Ave., Everett, WA 98201; 1-800-882-7860; *www.sunprecautions.com.*

American Center for Bicycle Registration, 3030 N. 3rd St., Suite 200, Phoenix, AZ 85012; (602) 241-8547.

National Bike Registry, 1832 Tribute Rd., Suite 205, Sacramento, CA 95815; 1-800-848-BIKE.

# Appendix 4

# State Bicycle/Pedestrian Coordinators

Five or ten minutes spent writing a short note to your state's bicycle/pedestrian coordinator can yield a wealth of free, useful information about bicycling with children. Some of the information you might request and receive includes:

- list of bicycle clubs in your state;
- brochures or lists of bicycle rodeos, fun rides, or other bicycling activities in the states;
- copy of your state's statutes and motor vehicle code regarding the rights and responsibilities of bicycles on the roads;
- copy of brochures, booklets, and coloring books on bicycling safety for children;
- maps of suggested

bicycle-touring routes in the state, and a list of published local ride guidebooks;

- bicycle-suitability maps or vehicle-traffic-flow maps useful in plotting your own day rides;
- a list of the freeways, limited-access highways, bridges, and tunnels that explicitly allow or prohibit bicyclists on their lanes or shoulders (useful for planning any statewide tour with older kids);
- brochures and booklets with practical, tested suggestions on encouraging bicycle commuting to reduce traffic and pollution (useful for teens and parents who want to try bicycling to and from work);
- a list of names, addresses, phone numbers of public transportation carriers (buses, subways, trains, etc.) that allow bicycles to be carried, with details about any permits that must be obtained and allowed hours the permits may be used (useful for touring or commuting).

Because people tend to shift in and out of jobs, no names are given for the people occupying the offices whose addresses are listed below. The names are, however, updated annually and are published each March in the Almanac issue of *Bicycle USA* (the magazine of the League of American Bicyclists; see Appendix 1 for address) and in *The Cyclists' Yellow Pages* (published by the Adventure Cycling Association; see Appendix 1 for address), both of which are available every year to members of each organization; single issues are available to nonmembers for a fee.

**Alabama**
Bicycle/Pedestrian Planner
Alabama Department of
   Transportation
1409 Coliseum Blvd.
Montgomery, AL 36130
(334) 242-6085
(334) 262-7658 (fax)

**Alaska**
Bicycle/Pedestrian Coordinator
Alaska Department of Transportation and Public Facilities
Division of Planning
3132 Channel Drive, Room 200
Juneau, AK 99801-7898
(907) 465-6975
(907) 465-6984 (fax)

**Arizona**
Bicycle/Pedestrian Coordinator
Transportation Planning Division
Arizona Department of
   Transportation
206 S. 17th Avenue, Suite 304B
Phoenix, AZ 85007
(602) 255-8010
(602) 256-7563 (fax)

# Bicycling with Children

**Arkansas**
Bicycle Coordinator
Planning Division
Highway and Transportation
  Department
P.O. Box 2261
Little Rock, AR 72203
(501) 569-2115
(501) 565-2476 (fax)

**California**
Office of Bicycle Facilities
California Department of
  Transportation (CALTRANS)
1120 N Street, Room 4500
P.O. Box 942874
Sacramento, CA 95814
(916) 653-0036
(916) 654-6583 (fax)

**Colorado**
Colorado Bicycle/Pedestrian
  Program Manager
Colorado Department of
  Highways
4201 E. Arkansas Avenue, Suite 255
Denver, CO 80222
(303) 757-9982

**Connecticut**
Bicycle Coordinator
Connecticut Department of
  Transportation
2800 Berlin Pike
P.O. Box 317546
Newington, CT 06131-3028
(203) 594-2145
(203) 594-3028 (fax)

**Delaware**
Bicycle/Pedestrian Coordinator

Delaware Department of
  Transportation
P.O. Box 778
Dover, DE 19903
(302) 739-2453
(302) 739-2251 (fax)

**District of Columbia**
Bicycle/Pedestrian Coordinator
D.C. Department of Public Works
2000 14th Street NW, 7th floor
Washington, D.C. 20009
(202) 939-8016
(202) 939-7185 (fax)

**Florida**
State Bicycle/Pedestrian
  Coordinator
Florida Department of
  Transportation
605 S. Suwannee Street, Mail
  Stop 82
Tallahassee, FL 32399-0450
(904) 487-1200
(904) 922-2935 (fax)

**Georgia**
Bicycle and Pedestrian Program
  Coordinator
Georgia Department of
  Transportation
2 Capitol Square, Room 345
Atlanta, GA 30334-1002
(404) 656-5427
(404) 656-3507 (fax)

**Hawaii**
Bicycle/Pedestrian Coordinator
Hawaii Department of
  Transportation
600 Kapiolani Blvd., Suite 410

Honolulu, HI 96813
(808) 587-2321
(808) 587-2325 (fax)

**Idaho**
Bicycle Coordinator
Idaho Department of
    Transportation
P.O. Box 7129
Boise, ID 83707-1129
(208) 334-8296
(208) 334-4432 (fax)

**Illinois**
Bikeway and Pedestrian
    Coordinator
Illinois Department of
    Transportation
2300 S. Dirksen Parkway, Room 330
Springfield, IL 62764
(217) 782-3194 or (217) 785-2148
(217) 524-9537 (fax)

**Indiana**
Bicycle/Pedestrian Coordinator
Planning Division
Indiana Department of
    Transportation
100 N. Senate Avenue, Room
    IGCN-901
Indianapolis, IN 46204-2249
(317) 232-5653
(317) 232-1499 (fax)

**Iowa**
Bicycle Program Coordinator
Iowa Department of Transportation
800 Lincoln Way
Ames, IA 50010
(515) 239-1621
(515) 239-1639 (fax)

**Kansas**
Bicycle Coordinator
Kansas Department of
    Transportation
Thacher Building, 2nd Floor
217 SE 4th Street
Topeka, KS 66603
(913) 296-7448
(913) 296-0963 (fax)

**Kentucky**
Bikeway and Pedestrian
    Coordinator
Division of Multimodal
    Programs
Kentucky Transportation Cabinet
Frankfort, KY 40622
(502) 564-7433
(502) 564-4422 (fax)

**Louisiana**
Bicycle/Pedestrian Coordinator
Louisiana Department of
    Transportation
P.O. Box 94245, Capitol Station
Baton Rouge, LA 70804-9245
(504) 358-9115
(504) 358-9160 (fax)

**Maine**
Bicycle and Pedestrian
    Coordinator
Office of Passenger
    Transportation
Maine Department of
    Transportation
16 State House Station
Augusta, ME 04333-0016
(207) 287-3318
(207) 287-8300 (fax)
e-mail: DTMVAND@state.me.us

**Maryland**
Bicycle and Pedestrian Coordinator
Maryland State Highway
  Administration
707 N. Calvert Street, Room 213
Baltimore, MD 21203-0717
(410) 545-5656
(410) 333-4999 (fax)
(800) 252-8776

**Massachusetts**
Bicycle-Pedestrian Program
  Coordinator
Massachusetts Highway
  Department
10 Park Plaza, Room 4150
Boston, MA 02116-3973
(617) 973-7329
(617) 973-8035 (fax)

**Michigan**
Non-Motorized Coordinator
Michigan Department of
  Transportation-Planning
P.O. Box 30050
Lansing, MI 48909
(517) 335-2823

**Minnesota**
State Bicycle Coordinator
Minnesota Department of
  Transportation
Transportation Building, Mail
  Stop 315
395 John Ireland Blvd.
St. Paul, MN 55155
(612) 297-1838
(612) 296-0509 (fax)

**Mississippi**
Transportation Planner

Mississippi Department of
  Transportation
P.O. Box 1850
Jackson, MS 39215-1850
(601) 359-7685
(601) 359-7652 (fax)

**Missouri**
Bicycle/Pedestrian Coordinator
Missouri Highway and
  Transportation Department
P.O. Box 270
Jefferson City, MO 65102
(314) 526-2816
(314) 426-2819 (fax)

**Montana**
Bicycle/Pedestrian Coordinator
Montana Department of
  Transportation
2701 Prospect Street
Helena, MT 59620
(406) 444-0809
(406) 444-7671 (fax)

**Nebraska**
Urban Planning and Liaison Unit
  and Bicycle/Pedestrian
  Coordinator
Transportation Planning Division
Nebraska Department of Roads
P.O. Box 94759
Lincoln, NE 68509-4759
(402) 479-4338
(402) 479-3884 (fax)

**Nevada**
Bicycle/Pedestrian Coordinator
Nevada Department of
  Transportation
Transportation Planning Division

# State Bicycle/Pedestrian Coordinators

1263 S. Stewart Street
Carson City, NV 89712
(702) 687-3022
(702) 687-1253 (fax)

**New Hampshire**
Bicycle/Pedestrian Transportation
   Coordinator
New Hampshire Department of
   Transportation
Bureau of Transportation Planning
P.O. Box 483
Concord, NH 03302-0483
(603) 271-3344
(603) 271-3914 (fax)

**New Jersey**
Pedestrian/Bicycle Advocate
New Jersey Department of
   Transportation
1035 Parkway Ave.
Trenton, NJ 08625
(609) 530-4578
(609) 530-8044 (fax)

**New Mexico**
Bicycle Coordinator
New Mexico Highway and
   Transportation Department
P.O. Box 1149
Santa Fe, NM 87504-1149
(505) 827-5248
(505) 989-4983 (fax)

**New York**
Bicycle/Pedestrian Program
   Manager
New York State Department of
   Transportation
1220 Washington Avenue
Building 4, Room 206

Albany, NY 12232-0424
(518) 457-8307
(518) 457-7960 (fax)

**North Carolina**
Director
Office of Bicycle and Pedestrian
   Transportation
North Carolina Department of
   Transportation
1 S. Wilmington Street, Room 422
P.O. Box 25201
Raleigh, NC 27611
(919) 733-2804
(919) 715-4422 (fax)

**North Dakota**
Bicycle/Pedestrian Coordinator
North Dakota State Department
   of Transportation
608 E. Boulevard Avenue
Bismarck, ND 58505-0700
(701) 328-4463
(701) 328-1404 (fax)

**Ohio**
Bicycle/Pedestrian Coordinator
Ohio Department of
   Transportation
25 S. Front Street, Room 707
Columbus, OH 43215
(614) 752-5359
(614) 752-6534 (fax)

**Oklahoma**
Bicycle Coordinator
Urban Design
Oklahoma Department of
   Transportation
200 NE 21st Street, Room 2-C2
Oklahoma City, OK 73105

(405) 521-2454
(405) 521-6528 (fax)

**Oregon**
Bicycle/Pedestrian Program
  Manager
Oregon Department of
  Transportation
Transportation Building, Room 210
Salem, OR 97310
(503) 986-3555
(503) 986-3896 (fax)
e-mail:michael.p.ronkin@state.or.us

**Pennsylvania**
Bicycle and Pedestrian Program
  Coordinator
Bureau of Highway Safety and
  Traffic Engineering
Pennsylvania Department of
  Transportation (PennDOT)
Box 2047, Room 203
Harrisburg, PA 17105-2047
(717) 783-8444
(717) 783-8012 (fax)

**Rhode Island**
Bicycle Coordinator
Planning Division
Rhode Island Department of
  Transportation Planning
2 Capitol Hill
State Office Building
Providence, RI 02903
(401) 277-2023
(401) 277-3435 (fax)

**South Carolina**
Bicycle/Pedestrian Coordinator
Traffic Engineering Department
South Carolina Department of

Transportation
P.O. Box 191
Columbia, SC 29202-0191
(803) 737-1052
(803) 737-0271 (fax)

**South Dakota**
Bicycle/Pedestrian Coordinator
Planning and Programming
South Dakota Department of
  Transportation
700 Broadway Avenue, E
Pierre, SD 57501-2586
(605) 773-3155
(605) 773-3921 (fax)

**Tennessee**
Transportation Manager
Tennessee Department of
  Transportation
James K. Polk Building, Suite 700
505 Deaderick Street
Nashville, TN 37243-0349
(615) 741-5310
(615) 741-2508 (fax)

**Texas**
Bicycle Coordinator
Texas Department of
  Transportation
Dewitt C. Greer State Highway
  Building
11th and Brazos
Austin, TX 78701-2483
(512) 416-3125
(512) 416-3161 (fax)

**Utah**
Bicycle/Pedestrian Coordinator
Program Development
Utah Department of

Transportation
4501 South 2700 West
Salt Lake City, UT 84119
(801) 965-3897
(801) 965-4551 (fax)

**Vermont**
Bicycle/Pedestrian Coordinator
Vermont Agency of
  Transportation
Division of RAPT
133 State St.
Montpelier, VT 05633
(802) 828-2711
(802) 828-2829 (fax)

**Virginia**
Transportation Planning Division
Virginia Department of
  Transportation
1401 E. Broad Street
Richmond, VA 23219
(804) 786-2964, 2985
(804) 225-4785 (fax)

**Washington**
Bicycle/Pedestrian Program
  Manager
Washington State Department of
  Transportation
P.O. Box 47393
Olympia, WA 98504-7393

(360) 753-7258
(360) 705-6815 (fax)

**West Virginia**
Bicycle/Pedestrian Coordinator
Division of Highways
West Virginia Department of
  Transportation
Building 5, Room A550
1900 Kanawha Street E
Charleston, WV 25305-0430
(304) 558-3069
(304) 448-1209 (fax)

**Wisconsin**
Bicycle/Pedestrian Coordinator
Wisconsin Department of
  Transportation
P.O. Box 7913
Madison WI 53707-7913
(608) 267-7757
(608) 267-0294 (fax)

**Wyoming**
Bicycle/Pedestrian Coordinator
Building 6263
Wyoming Department of
  Transportation
P.O. Box 1708
Cheyenne, WY 82003-1708
(307) 777-4719
(307) 777-4759 (fax)

# Acknowledgments

Every book is the product of many hands and minds. This one is no exception. Chronologically first, I wish to thank Laura Strom of Globe Pequot Press for suggesting I contact Margaret Foster at The Mountaineers Books with my proposal for this book—and Margaret for her enthusiastic reception of it. I also thank Cindy Bohn and others at The Mountaineers for their work and good suggestions.

I wish to thank the following people for hours of interviews either in person or by phone. Even though not all are cited by name elsewhere in the book, their contributions were vital to its fabric: Harry Baker of Santa Cruz, California, one of the coleaders of Youth Bicycle Education Network; Greg Combs of Colorado Springs, Colorado, a doctoral candidate in sports management at the University of Northern Colorado in Greeley, focusing on human rehabilitation support and services, and an elite license cycling coach at the U.S. Olympic Center; John Cooper of Pasadena, California, father of blind preteen Eliza who rides stoker on her Dad's tandem, and enjoys camping and rock climbing; Mark Garlikov of Dayton, Ohio, who pioneered three days of kids' rides offered at the League of American Bicyclists' rally in Dayton in July 1996; Steve Heinrichs, physical education teacher for twenty-three years in Dayton, Ohio, who designed a balance harness; Jeff Leahy of Cincinnati, Ohio, father of a boy with muscular dystrophy who has enjoyed riding in the [Des Moines] *Register* Annual Great Bicycle Ride Across Iowa (RAGBRAI) as a result of his father's converting his wheelchair into a crude bicycle rickshaw; Bonnie McClun, of the League of American Bicyclists, Washington, D.C., for her discussions on the League's Kids I, II, and III programs; Carol Minges, teacher of multiply handicapped students at Belmont High School in Dayton, Ohio, and Harold Jones of Huber Heights, Ohio, who together run bicycling adventures for the students in the Camp COPE (Challenging Outdoor Physical Encounters) summer program; John P. Waterman, founder and director of The Arc Cycling Program for disabled children and adults in Wayne, Michigan.

I also wish to thank the bicycle mechanics who devoted their time to showing me equipment and sharing their expertise in topics ranging from the quality of equipment to teaching kids to ride: Vaux Hall Cyclery, Maplewood, New Jersey; Pat Driscoll, Millburn Bike Shop, Millburn, New Jersey.; Brad Ford, formerly head mechanic at Cheapskates/The Cycle Pros in South Orange and Orange, New Jersey; Rich

Politz, co-owner of two Bikesport shops in Harleysville and Trappe, Pennsylvania. Thanks also for the copious information posted on the websites of bike shop owners Sheldon Brown of Harris Cyclery, Stephen M. Ciccarelli of Falls Church, Va., and others.

My gratitude also goes to the following e-mail correspondents and other individuals for their useful observations, mailed materials, and generous offers of help in response to classified ads I placed in various bicycling magazines: Herb Alfasso; Steve Baker of New Jersey and California; Hal "Bikerak"; Wade Blomgren; Aaron Blum of Canton, Massachusetts; "Bob in Edmonton"; Peter Boor (Effective Cycling Instructor #4); Jeff Breshears; Martin Cooperman; Gayle Ellis Davis of the Girl Scouts of America in New York City; Tom Diskin of San Mateo, Calif.; Dave Franzen of Mount Kisco, New York; Allen Freeman of Meriden, Connecticut; Richard Gould; Jeffrey Gruttz; Michael Howell of the University of British Columbia; Richard Jorgensen of Davis, California; John Kennedy of the U.S. Bicycle Polo Association, Sacramento, Calif.; Michael Lampi; Al Lauland; Mark Q. Lee of Frankfort, Kentucky; Ellen Metrick of the National Lekotek Center, Evanston, Ill.; Edie Miller of Arlington, Massachusetts; David Mozer of the International Bicycle Fund in Seattle, Washington; Judy Murphy of Juneau, Alaska; John Overstreet of Severn, Maryland; Steve Rankin; David E. Reed of Niantic, Connecticut; hhstokes@uic.edu; Jean Seay; Joe Siebert of Children's Hospital and Medical Center in Seattle, Washington; msnit@juno.com; Marietta and David Swain; Randy Swart of the Bicycle Helmet Safety Institute; Dick at *www.cycletote.com*; Brad Taylor of Salisbury, Maryland; John Waltz (ECI #138); Bell Mead, New Jersey; Unesential@aol.com; and Lee Weisman. If I have inadvertently missed anyone, please accept my apologies and thanks—and let me know about my oversight.

I am especially grateful to the following interviewees who were so generous with their time and so frank about their own experiences in bicycling as children and adults despite their physical disabilities. I appreciate their unanimous, passionate advice to other children and parents to go for it: Cindy Wright Hammond of Chelmsford, Massachusetts; T. C. Hulsey, of Napa, California; M. J. Lowe of Statesboro, Georgia; Richard and Karen Mayberry and their son, Joe, and daughter, Kathryn, of Lansdale, Pennsylvania, for their hospitality over Memorial Day weekend in 1997, and for all Richard's time spent showing me all he knows about tandems, trailers, and bicycling with blind stokers.

I also thank Donald Tighe, former editor of the League of American Bicyclists' magazine, *Bicycle USA*, in Washington, D.C., for publishing two articles that evolved into sections of this book, and for all the time

# Bicycling with Children

he has spent sharing with me his observations on bicycling adults and children as well as his extensive helpful (and humorous) feedback and encouragement. I also thank the parents, teens, and children who attended the focus group discussion I convened early in the project to learn what they would like to see covered in a book on bicycling with children. A tip of the helmet to Mary Dodd, Arlean Lambert, Barbara Novack, Nelson Rodriguez, Jessica, Colin, and David Tuck, Bill and Sue Canis, and especially Craig B. Waff—who also suggested I write the pioneering section on bicycling for children with challenges.

Thanks are due to the parents and children who served as photographic models, especially Grace Saccardi (and her mom, Sue) and my nephew, Kenneth Henderson Bell (and his mom, Shanna). Also, thanks to all the unknown parents and children I have watched in parks and public places, either bicycling with their children or teaching them to ride, for all the lessons they have taught me.

Thanks are due to the various photographic laboratories I've used, and their helpful and patient staffs: Eddie and his crew at Graphic Lab in New York City; Pro-Lab Northwest, Inc. in Portland, Oregon; and Ritz Camera One-Hour Photo in the Galleria Building in Cleveland, Ohio (especially to manager Kevin Lytle and to Margaleet Sweeney).

Special thanks are due to Steven P. Schwarzwaelder and the entire Operational Effectiveness Development Team at McKinsey & Company, for granting me an unpaid leave—even though I had less than six months' tenure in my new position—to finish this book manuscript in time to meet its contractual deadline. Special thanks are also due to my mother, Arabella J. Bell, and my daughter's nanny, Edith Magaña, for caring for my daughter when I needed uninterrupted hours to write, and to my mother, again, for proofreading the manuscript.

The greatest thanks of all are due my beloved daughter and coauthor, Roxana Katharine Bell, for all her good nature in being the subject of Mama's endless study and photography, as well as for making solid suggestions and contributions of her own to this book. May we continue to enjoy many day rides, bike camping trips, and coauthorships together!

*Trudy E. Bell*

# INDEX

# Bicycling with Children

# ABOUT THE AUTHORS

Trudy E. Bell has traveled by bicycle in the mid-Atlantic states and New England as well as in Colorado, Ohio, Utah, California, and along the length of Baja California. She has taught courses on bicycle touring for adults and is a certified bicycle mechanic.The author of *The Essential Bicycle Commuter, The Best Bike Rides in the Mid-Atlantic,* and *Bicycling Around New York City: A Gentle Touring Guide,* she has also published articles in *The New York Times, Essence, Adventure Cyclist, Bicycle USA,* and *The Bicyclist's Sourcebook.* She lives in Lakewood, Ohio, with her daughter and coauthor Roxana K. Bell, who was introduced to bicycling at the age of twenty months.

THE MOUNTAINEERS, founded in 1906, is a nonprofit outdoor activity and conservation club, whose mission is "to explore, study, preserve, and enjoy the natural beauty of the outdoors . . . . " Based in Seattle, Washington, the club is now the third-largest such organization in the United States, with 15,000 members and five branches throughout Washington State.

The Mountaineers sponsors both classes and year-round outdoor activities in the Pacific Northwest, which include hiking, mountain climbing, ski-touring, snowshoeing, bicycling, camping, kayaking and canoeing, nature study, sailing, and adventure travel. The club's conservation division supports environmental causes through educational activities, sponsoring legislation, and presenting informational programs. All club activities are led by skilled, experienced volunteers, who are dedicated to promoting safe and responsible enjoyment and preservation of the outdoors.

If you would like to participate in these organized outdoor activities or the club's programs, consider a membership in The Mountaineers. For information and an application, write or call The Mountaineers, Club Headquarters, 300 Third Avenue West, Seattle, Washington 98119; (206) 284-6310.

The Mountaineers Books, an active, nonprofit publishing program of the club, produces guidebooks, instructional texts, historical works, natural history guides, and works on environmental conservation. All books produced by The Mountaineers are aimed at fulfilling the club's mission.

**Send or call for our catalog of more than 300 outdoor titles:**

 The Mountaineers Books
1001 SW Klickitat Way, Suite 201
Seattle, WA 98134
1-800-553-4453
e-mail: mbooks@mountaineers.org
website: www.mountaineersbooks.org

Other titles you may enjoy from The Mountaineers:

**BEST HIKES WITH CHILDREN® Series:**
**Best Hikes with Children in Colorado, Second Ed.,** *Maureen Keilty*
**Best Hikes with Children in Connecticut, Massachusetts, and Rhode Island, Second Ed.,** *Cynthia C. Lewis & Thomas J. Lewis*
**Best Hikes with Children in Western Washington & The Cascades, Volumes 1 & 2, Second Eds.,** *Joan Burton*
**Best Hikes with Children in Pennsylvania,** *Sally Trepanowski*
**Best Hikes with Children around Sacramento,** *Bill McMillon*
*Plus TEN more titles!*
Fifteen guidebooks to day hikes and overnighters for families throughout the U.S., including the Southwest and Pacific Northwest, New England, and the Mid-Atlantic states. Includes tips on hiking with kids, safety, and fostering a wilderness ethic. Each book features points of interest, trail descriptions, information on flora and fauna, campsite locations, and maps.

**OUTDOOR FAMILY GUIDE Series:**
**An Outdoor Family Guide to Acadia National Park,** *Lisa Gollin Evans*
**An Outdoor Family Guide to Rocky Mountain National Park, Second Ed.,** *Lisa Gollin Evans*
**Lake Tahoe: A Family Guide,** *Lisa Gollin Evans*
**An Outdoor Family Guide to the Southwest's Four Corners,** *Tom & Gayen Wharton*
**An Outdoor Family Guide to Washington's National Parks & Monument,** *Vicky Spring & Tom Kirkendall*
**An Outdoor Family Guide to Yellowstone & Grand Teton National Parks,** *Lisa Gollin Evans*
Comprehensive, multi-season guides to the best selection of outdoor activities in several regions throughout the U.S.

**KIDS IN THE WILD: A Family Guide to Outdoor Recreation,** *Cindy Ross & Todd Gladfelter*
A family-tested handbook of advice on sharing outdoor adventures with children of all ages and skill levels, with recommendations on equipment, food, safety, and family activities.